How To Borrow Money

Stephen M. Pollan

and

Raymond A. Roel and Ronald E. Roel

Cornerstone Library
Published by Simon & Schuster
New York

Published by Cornerstone Library,
A Simon & Schuster Division of Gulf & Western Corporation
Simon & Schuster Building
1230 Avenue of the Americas
New York, New York 10020
CORNERSTONE LIBRARY and colophon are trademarks of
Simon & Schuster, registered in the U.S. Patent and Trademark Office.

Designed by: *Judy Allan (The Designing Woman)*

10 9 8 7 6 5 4 3 2 1

Manufactured in the United States of America

Library of Congress Cataloging in Publication Data

Pollan, Stephen M.
  How to borrow money.

  "Cornerstone Library."
  Includes index.
  1. Consumer credit—Handbooks, manuals, etc.
2. Credit—Handbooks, manuals, etc. 3. Credit bureaus—
Handbooks, manuals, etc. I. Roel, Ronald E. II. Roel,
Raymond A. III. Title.
HG3755.P63   1983   332.7′43   82-19683

ISBN 0-346-12546-4

Contents

The Big Picture
The Last Word

Appendix B   **Where to Push the Up Button**   208

Appendix C   **Major U.S. Credit Bureaus**   211

             Glossary   226

             Index   237

Acknowledgments

In writing this book we were guided by many people who helped us take charge of our own ideas. We especially want to thank the following people and organizations for their generous time and assistance: William Davidson, Dahlia Fernandez, Joseph P. Frey, Deborah Harkins, Barbara Herndon, Marvin and Frances Kaplan, Anita McClellan, Corky Pollan, Michael Pollan, Robert Pollan, Edmund and Adele Roel, Anthony Sisti, Frank Wolf, Associated Credit Bureaus, Credit Research Center at Purdue University, Credit Union National Association, National Association of Bank Women.

Why
We Wrote
This Book

TAKE CHARGE OF YOUR CREDIT. THIS SIMPLE MESSAGE—GETTING involved to improve your credit potential and borrowing money in order to lead a fuller life—emerged from the stories of people across America who shared with me and my coauthors their questions and fears and actual experiences with credit and borrowing today.

Throughout my career as a lawyer, venture capitalist, commercial banker, and consumer, I have learned a bit about the consumer credit industry from a few perspectives. But it's only been since I became a business professor and subsequently began touring the country talking to students about credit that I truly started to grasp the enormity of our problem with credit. Moreover, teaching the American Express credit lecture series brought me into contact with growing spheres of credit-anxious people. I've had the benefit of listening to and trying to help troubled callers on many television and radio talk shows; I continue to get responses after offering consumer tips about credit and banking on television—everywhere (large cities and small towns) I've gone, I have found a vacuum of knowledge about credit.

With the additional extensive research done by my coauthors, I have learned that there is a vast, secret reservoir of credit fear. In our doubts about the ways of borrowing we are all alone together.

This book was written to satisfy a tremendous desire for knowledge. It is designed to demystify credit and the borrowing process, to show you that, viewed and used properly, credit becomes an invaluable life skill to better every stage of your life. Credit is here; it's available; it's a fact of life, both abused and underused. Everyone needs to know about credit, but, like sex, it is not being taught in the classroom. It's time to take credit out of the closet. This book will illuminate many of the misconceptions and bad techniques still all too common in the credit world, separating facts from fantasy.

The rules that govern the business of living seem to be changing rapidly. High interest rates, fears of renewed inflation, and high unemployment among workers in the old industrial backbone of this country have combined to create a huge, huddled mass of frustrated Americans—the new "have-nots." And many more of us are being forced to postpone or abandon the traditional goals of buying a new car, owning a new home, or sending our children to the best schools. Everywhere we look, the chances for consumer loans seem slim; credit is as tight as last year's jeans, and we really don't know how to present our case to potential lenders.

This book will help you become more creditworthy and increase your borrowing quotient. We do not offer a blanket recommendation to borrow at any price. In fact, we warn you to stay away from a host of different credit con artists. But we also acknowledge that we all need credit to keep the old dreams alive, to survive and succeed in the United States today.

Face it: Credit is more than money. It has become a measurement of your character and good name, and is increasingly being used as a criterion in job hiring and career advancement.

This book is not a "how-to" listing of credit laws and facts. It's true we supply a good deal of information concerning procedure that we know has proven helpful to others. But *How to Borrow Money* is a chronicle of people like you, who have confronted their own credit fears as well as the corporate world of credit requirements, and learned how to use credit and borrowing to their best advantage. Our aim is to rehumanize the credit granting process, build your credit confidence, and help you reach out for a better life.

Stephen M. Pollan
Ronald E. Roel
Raymond A. Roel

New York
October 25, 1982.

Chapter One

The Myth
and Reality
of Borrowing

GROWING UP IN THE BRONX DURING THE NEW DEAL, I WIT-
nessed the same distressing scene every Sunday night. Sitting at the kitchen table, my father, the butter-and-eggs
salesman, would carefully tally the payments due the next
day against what little remained from his Friday paycheck.
It never seemed to balance. He was always one week behind, and invariably I would hear the same exasperating
question: "Why does this always happen to us?" Every
Monday, my father would go to Uncle Harry to see if he
could "borrow a week," with the promise that he would be
repaid out of next Friday's paycheck. (Harry was a bache-
lor; he could afford it.) This went on for 10 years: a weekly
ritual of shame and humiliation that plagued my parents
needlessly and made an indelible impression on me.

At that stage in their lives, my parents considered banks
to be impenetrable; the banks were not in business to lend
money to people like my parents, or so they thought. The
whole idea of borrowing from strangers was cloaked in fear
and dread of being "enslaved" by demanding creditors.
Even when my parents finally relented and went to a per-

sonal finance company, the borrowing environment was hardly better—those were the days of small and seedy second-floor walkup offices.

The misconceptions of my parents about borrowing are widespread and deeply ingrained in many societies and have been since ancient times, when the penalty for failure to meet a debt was enslavement. This grim prospect—or the specter of imprisonment—haunted borrowers over many centuries, and so wise counselors warned against it. Benjamin Franklin, in *The Way to Wealth,* summed up the age-old wisdom: "He who goes a-borrowing goes a-sorrowing."

Even today, when default means neither imprisonment nor slavery, many people view the need to borrow as a sign of a precarious financial position at best, a state of desperation at worst. Borrowing, after all, can lead to the harassment of creditors, to foreclosures and repossessions, to runaway credit card spending, even to bankruptcy. For many, taking out a loan is a disgrace, a form of gluttony, a servile act.

But just as there are risks in borrowing, there are consequences in *not* borrowing: the apartment not purchased, the trip not taken, the college education denied, the business not started, the inability to borrow for dire emergencies—in short, the constricted life. There are good, positive reasons to borrow: to improve your lifestyle and productivity, to acquire a hedge against inflation, to develop the creditworthiness that will prepare you for financial opportunities and emergencies. Skillful borrowing is a powerful tool, a managerial asset that should last a lifetime. This book will help you acquire that valuable asset.

BORROWING TO IMPROVE THE QUALITY OF YOUR LIFE

People usually go through life waiting for certain things to happen at certain times. You wait until you are married, and often for a number of years after you get married, before buying a home. You wait until you have saved enough money before buying the second home, the boat, the trailer, the pool. You wait until you retire before taking the trips you've always wanted.

Borrowing lets you accelerate your life, lets you "trade up," jump ahead without having to wait. If it helps to improve the productivity and quality of your life, you *should* borrow. Borrowing allows you to "leverage" yourself into a higher lifestyle. Buying a better home in a better neighborhood; providing a better education for your children; getting a much needed and culturally rewarding vacation—these are valid reasons to borrow money. The prudent use of credit allows you, in a manner of speaking, to take a bite out of the apple before you lose your teeth.

Borrowing for "life"—where the yield is happiness and productivity—is an essential part of our social fabric and economic philosophy. We borrow books that we cannot afford from libraries; we borrow blood from blood banks; we borrow money, as the public, to build museums and galleries to house paintings, artifacts, and culture that we can't all have individually.

Corporations, too, have a long-established tradition of creating their own readiness to do things by borrowing money. They borrow through banks, bond offerings, and commercial paper to upgrade plants and equipment, develop new products, create new jobs, and increase productivity. Business borrows to invest. It does not wait for opportunities, but follows its own internal readiness, negotiating loans based upon expectancy of future income made possible through borrowing. Ironically, John Ruskin, the nineteenth-century art critic, who once wrote that "borrowers are nearly always ill spenders," also gave us the reason for good borrowing: "There is no wealth but life."

Consumer borrowing, as much as corporate borrowing, should be thought of as an *investment* in long-term gains. When you borrow to buy a house or to put your son or daughter through college, you are investing in long-term equity or lifetime employment skills. But long-term investment also includes borrowing to buy quality merchandise: buying better things that last longer is a sound investment. Today, because of chronic inflation, borrowing often has proven to be a sensible way to invest. From the viewpoint of strict arithmetic, buying now with borrowed money works if the price of an item increases more than the financing charge during the loan period. And not only are you enjoying immediate ownership while paying back cheaper dollars; in buying better quality items you are saving the cost of replacing cheaper merchandise, whose price naturally increases year after year in an inflationary economy.

Borrowing enables you to enjoy the quality of life that you would miss by not developing your credit. This does not imply that there is no sacrifice involved, no substantial interest to be paid. It means that as long as you borrow at a rate less than your total yield in value, quality, future productivity, and happiness, you are using borrowing as an effective investment tool. Once again, like the businessperson who uses borrowing as an investment leverage against inflation, the consumer can use borrowing as a hedge against the erosion of inflation, converting present liabilities into future assets. Even in an environment where certain aspects of inflation have subsided somewhat, other costs continue unabated: college, residential construction, and medical care, to name just a few.

BORROWING FOR THE POWER OF CREDIT

Borrowing—the use of credit—is the most important factor in the creation of creditworthiness. Your credit rating today has become much more than a simple measure of how much you can borrow from a bank, department store, or oil company. Credit is a validation of your character, a quantitative measure of your trustworthiness. Good credit is power, both economic and social; it can be as critical in getting a good job as in getting into a good club. Just having credit gives you a sense of self-esteem and confidence. It is a statement about your stability and standing in your community—"he's a man of his word, he pays his bills." In an uncertain, volatile, inflationary economy, the fear of not having money is a real, throbbing presence. Having good credit gives us options through borrowing; it keeps alive our potential to hope for a richer life.

While good credit is undeniably a valuable asset, it is also one that we most often leave unattended. We are inclined to let the banks and other creditors decide on our creditworthiness; most of us still don't really participate in the credit-making process.

Credit is something that should not be taken for granted. I'll never forget the incredulous look on the face of a Georgetown coed when I told her that her family's wealth had nothing to do with her own credit. She was appalled that it could not be taken care of for her. There is no way to get around the fact that you must demonstrate *your own* ability and willingness to repay debts to validate your credit. Quite apart from the accumulation of money, credit is an individually developed characteristic that cannot be inherited.

Conventional wisdom supposes that credit is like yogurt—you have to have some already in order to get some more. But you can be your own "starter." Through careful, well-planned borrowing and overall care of credit, you can create a credit profile that puts you in a position to handle problems and take advantage of opportunities as they arise. Your borrowing can not only leverage your lifestyle, but it can help build your credit for that unforeseen "rainy day."

When I graduated from law school years ago and first established my own practice, I confidently decided one lunch hour to walk over to a local bank and apply for a new-car loan. It was my first loan: I shouldn't have any problem, I thought, as I proudly wrote out the word "lawyer" under occupation. It was a shock to my system when I was rejected. I felt humiliated and empty; how could they do this to me? With my wounded ego still smarting, I listened in astonishment to an apologetic loan officer carefully explain that it was against the bank's policy to make loans to people who had no credit. My ready response of, "But that's why I'm here—to get credit," moved him not at all.

This was a moment of truth—to last forever—that credit could be a "Catch-22," available when you already have it.

THEY WANT YOUR BUSINESS

The business of lending is no longer the clear-cut, conservative profession it once was. With the passage of the Depository Institutions Deregulation and Monetary Control Act in 1980, Congress ushered in a new era of free-market competition to the banking industry. Banks and other financial institutions, including insurance companies, finance companies, major retailers, and manufacturers, will be engaged in a protracted battle for your business in the eighties. In fact, the definition of what a bank is has become unclear, with giant "near-banks" like Sears Roebuck, GE, American Express, and Merrill Lynch enjoying the ability to extend consumer credit and lend money freely without the constraints affecting banks.

Most industry analysts agree that, within a few years, the Douglas Amendment to the McFadden Act will be revised to allow commercial banks to conduct business, including the issuing of loans, outside their original home state. Anticipating this change, the larger banks are buying finance companies whose offices can be quickly converted into deposit-taking branches and full-service banks when the prohibition is eased. Conversely, finance companies are buying up banks and thrift institutions as they try to shift their entire customer base from the indigent to the affluent. The larger finance companies like Household Finance, Beneficial, and Creditthrift Financial are diversifying their services, trying to overcome their image as lenders to those unable to borrow elsewhere, hoping to phase out their smaller (under $500) unprofitable consumer loan programs and capture a portion of the huge market of upscale, low-risk borrowers.

As the competition thickens and intensifies, companies may well be willing to sacrifice short-term profits in order to penetrate the national consumer market and increase their market share over the long term. The stakes are huge. A shift in a single percentage point of business will represent hundreds of millions of dollars for many of the larger companies. The weaker financial institutions will fail, especially many beleaguered savings and loan associations that have been caught in a profit squeeze, paying high interest rates for today's money while being committed to past low-interest, long-term mortgage loans. Some analysts predict that in the next ten years the nation's 14,000 banks will shrink to half that number.

It is important for you, the consumer, to be aware of the tremendous volatility in the banking market—"how it is out there"—because it represents new opportunities and pitfalls for you as a borrower and planner of your financial affairs. The proliferation of competitive banking services is eroding the commercial banker's traditional marketing premise: customer loyalty. The bankers of the eighties will increasingly recognize that the cost-conscious, savvy consumer will shop around to compare rates before settling on a bank. After all, why should you borrow from your regular bank if the bank across the street offers you a better deal? Bankers will have to make special efforts to market themselves, to reestablish that personal sense of caring and trust that traditionally fostered your loyalty to a particular bank. With their equity-to-assets ratio stretched to the limit, banks will be aggressively pursuing your business, reaching out for your recommendation. Now, more than ever, the banks need you; you are an important customer.

THE BASICS OF BORROWING

While borrowing money in the next decade should seem more of a "right" than a mere privilege, consumers must still learn to prepare themselves properly to obtain the loans they want and need. To be successful, you must be aware of how creditors evaluate you and your loan application; you must know what these creditors are looking for and how they want you to present yourself. In every step of the borrowing process, you must be prepared.

Bankers in the United States traditionally have referred to the "three Cs of credit"—character, capacity, and collateral (not necessarily in that order)—as their admittedly subjective method of determining creditworthiness. Through experience they have spun off other old slogans: "Never lend to beauticians, bartenders, or barbers" or "Never lend to preachers, plumbers, or prostitutes." (It seems that the bankers' limits in terms of alliteration and bad-risk evaluation rest at three.) The bank's analysis of your credit—your ability to pay back a loan—is based on the principle that past experience predicts future performance; people tend to behave consistently. In reviewing your loan application, the banker examines his or her bank's experience with repayment of loans in situations similar to your own. Loan officers are instructed to be conservative, because the loss from one default usually far exceeds the profits accrued from a successful loan.

Credit analysis has been, and continues to be, a subjective judgment call. You get a loan if your banker believes you have both the ability and the inclination to pay it back. But since the mid-1960s, financial institutions and other creditors have been applying, with increasing frequency, a "credit-scoring" system to appraise the creditworthiness of loan applicants. Your "objective criteria" (length of time at present job, number of years at present address, etc.) are given numerical scores by low-level bank employees who mechanically process your loan application. Your aggregate score is measured against a computer model reflecting the bank's past experience with both successful and unsuccessful loans. Your score is then translated into a supposedly exact probability of repayment, allowing the banker to select the assumed degree of risk that he or she is willing to accept when approving any loan. It is the New Math of borrowing, and it promises to eliminate guesswork. In fact, it threatens to eliminate human analysis and contact—to deny the loan applicant any chance of persuading the banker of his creditworthiness.

No longer does a skilled loan officer have to wade through every application. Only those earning a certain score merit his attention. By reducing credit analysis to a scoring system, an unlimited number of applicants can be processed by clerks. And with the further consolidation of banking institutions, economies of scale will allow more firms to develop their own computer models and financial data bases. In this scenario, credit bureau agencies and credit scoring will continue to grow because they increase the bank's ability to do business at low costs, thus increasing its profit margin.

You need not submit to being a passive, faceless loan applicant. You can get the attention of someone in authority, if you fill out your loan application properly. (Chapters 4 and 5 will show you how to do so.)

Additional help comes in the form of consumer legislation enacted in the seventies to protect the loan applicant from the vagaries of some scoring systems and credit bureau processes. The Equal Credit Opportunity Act and the Consumer Credit Protection Act and their revisions, along with the Federal Reserve Board's further regulation, guarantee you certain rights and also require banks and credit agencies to follow nondiscriminatory procedures.

While the specific methodologies employed by banks in credit scoring are often proprietary and confidential, they are undergoing scrutiny and debate within the industry and by the Federal Reserve Board, and are subject to court challenges. In short, you often do have recourse.

The following chapters will guide you through the specifics of your loan application and explain to you the many options that come with credit. We will show you how to manipulate the "objective" criteria to make them work to your advantage and, where need be, show you how to circumvent them entirely.

Paying attention to details while shepherding your application through its various stages is often critical in obtaining your loan. I recently met an assistant vice president at a large commercial bank who had suffered the humiliation of being turned down for a loan from her own bank. She had been in the midst of a divorce and had not bothered to mention to anyone that she was filing the application. She had not, therefore, had the advantage of personally discussing her qualifications with a senior officer. A clerk tabulated her score, which was summarily declared below the acceptable level of creditworthiness. The "mistake" was eventually fixed, but it illustrates the point that anything can happen if you remain a passive receptacle of a bank's system of accreditation.

Finally, obtaining credit and borrowing money cannot be accomplished effectively in a state of fear. A cordial attitude toward your banker and, more important, your own self-esteem are the most critical qualifications you can bring to the bank.

In my years as a senior lending officer for a large commercial bank, I actually heard people *apologize* for applying for their loans. I could only respond, "That's what we're in business for!" But any banker worth his three-piece suit quickly learns to smell fear and becomes wary. The fact is that while borrowing is more of a right than a privilege today, you must prepare yourself properly and present your case in accordance with the banker's laundry list of objective criteria if you want to get your loan. The first step is to satisfy *yourself* that you are worthy of the loan: you must avoid the insecurities of my father, who was a solid citizen and a reliable wage earner, but who missed many of the opportunities that credit affords because he never knew his own worth.

Making
Credit
Bureaus
Your Ally

A THRIVING YET LARGELY INVISIBLE INDUSTRY EXERCISES A vast amount of power over you. Your ability to get a loan, your career advancement, your life insurance, even the basis for your acceptance into a country club can all be tied in part to your credit rating. Your credit report or profile is fast becoming the standard quantification of your character, respectability, and importance—either a "Good Housekeeping" seal of approval or a scarlet letter of rejection.

No longer is the letter of reference from your clergyman or other community leader of much interest to your banker (unless he is willing to sign as a guarantor). The time-honored process of sitting down with a loan officer for a face-to-face evaluation is being usurped by a computer printout. Quite simply, your credit bureau report has become the single most important tool with which businesses judge you.

Without your knowledge or active assent, any number of the country's more than 1,900 consumer rating agencies—commonly called credit bureaus—may possess a file on your history of repaying loans and credit and charge card obligations. Many of these companies are remarkably resourceful in obtaining the most minute details concerning an individual's credit repayment patterns plus other personal data. Even the smaller, local credit bureaus are rushing to convert to computerized operations that allow them access to the centralized computer files of a national credit bureau with its data on millions of individuals.

From these files, a credit bureau can produce for a requesting subscriber to its services—let's say your bank—a revealing report about your past and present credit activity. Business customers of TRW Credit Data, the nation's largest consumer credit reporting agency, for example, can receive an individual's credit profile through a video terminal or a printout within three to 10 seconds from the time of inquiry. While there are many legal restrictions and company policies governing the use of this information, approximately 200 million such reports on individuals are being generated annually in the United States.

We frequently encounter people who act outraged upon learning about the credit bureau business and challenge their authority to compile consumer files. "What right do they have to store and sell all of this personal information about me without my consent?" The facts are that you give the credit grantor the right when you sign any application for credit. It's in the small print.

In the course of teaching "How to Borrow" seminars to the general public in New York City recently, I constantly dealt with people being intimidated by credit bureaus, regarded as the mechanistic incarnation of "Big Brother." After class, credit-anxious people (from every strata of society) pulled me aside and furtively showed me their terse and bewildering computer printout credit report. Many had been rejected for bank loans and viewed their negatively coded credit profile as the automated culprit.

It is a natural reaction. After all, credit reports are treated by many businesses today like fiscal report cards—silent yet tangible records of your supposed performance. Worse, they can be damning indictments of your integrity,

black marks that can haunt you for years, effectively inhib-
iting your growth and ability to achieve your life goals.
Credit bureaus have inordinate memories; they operate by
calendars that are unforgiving; and their presentation of the
"facts" can unfairly precipitate your condemnation in the
eyes of the bank's loan officer or other creditors.

You can, however, override the normal dynamics of the
credit reporting system as it operates today and make it
work for you. By attending to the following procedures,
you can effectively "humanize" your credit profile and, in
the process, make the credit bureau your ally.

Before you interview your banker to discuss your plans,
before you even fill out your loan application, you should
seek out the various credit bureaus that have you on their
files, make any necessary corrections, and elaborate on
your credit credentials.

HOW CREDIT BUREAUS WORK

In order to break through and be heard in today's system
of computerized credit reporting, you must understand the
beast.

A credit bureau, or credit reporting agency, is simply any
business that collects consumer credit information from
other businesses that extend credit, as well as from other
sources, official and otherwise, and in turn sells this information back to its customers.

Credit bureaus do not grant credit. They are merely purveyors of facts—your record of payments to all businesses
reporting to them. Every time you receive a bill from a reporting business—a department store, mail order house, or
bank credit card—somewhere a credit bureau will shortly
receive your name, address, social security number, account number, marital status, amount, type, and terms of
the particular credit. Subsequent months will log how long
it took you to pay, what your balance is, and what your
credit limit is. In addition, a number of credit bureaus rou-

tinely scan public court records and enter into your files if you have been sued, divorced, or convicted of a crime, if you have not paid taxes, or if you have filed for bankruptcy. Your occupation, employer's name, gross annual income, and number of dependents—often out of date—are other bits of information that some of the credit bureaus pick up and that are included in your credit profile.

Certain information should not find its way into your file and can be removed under most circumstances. Specifically, any information relating to your arrest on a criminal charge should immediately be expunged from your record, *unless* you have a criminal conviction for such offense or the charges are still pending. Any negative information in your files more than seven years old must be deleted from your credit report, except for bankruptcy, which can remain on your record for 10 years. Although Congress and the Federal Trade Commission have done much in the last decade to regulate and police credit bureaus, the burden of keeping your credit profile accurate and current still rests with you. The credit bureaus are not liable for errors, except for malicious misdeeds.

The development and growth of credit bureaus is directly related to the encouragement of consumer credit in the United States by consumer-related businesses. From 1960 to 1982 alone, consumer borrowing mushroomed from $56 billion to $340 billion—approximately $1,500 of debt for every living person in the country.

In order for companies to screen out the notorious deadbeats from their good customers, they needed access to consumer repayment information. Businesses first met this demand in the early 1900s by gathering their own customers' repayment records and exchanging them with other branches of their firm, and sometimes also with other companies in the same industry. At first the records were stored in a central location in paper files. When the burgeoning volume of credit information threatened to outstrip an individual company's ability to cope, merchant loan exchanges were born to meet the need. They amassed consumer loan repayment histories and made them available to merchant members within a particular industry.

Soon the desire by local businesses to know a consumer's repayment profile spanning several industries spawned the credit bureau. Among the many bureaus was the former Michigan Merchant Credit Association, which changed its name to Credit Data Corp. and, in 1965, was the first to install a computerized, on-line credit reporting system. It was subsequently bought by TRW Inc. in 1969, and became TRW Credit Data.

Today TRW is the largest single credit bureau in the United States, with information on more than 80 million consumers, plugging into 24,000 business subscribers at 35,000 locations. The other giants of the industry include Trans Union, servicing approximately 80 million consumers through ten offices nationwide and associations with more than 125 other local credit bureaus; Pinger, based in Houston; Chilton, based in Dallas; and Credit Bureau Inc. (CBI), a subsidiary of Equifax, based in Atlanta. With the exception of TRW and a few others, these credit bureaus are all members of the Associated Credit Bureaus, Inc., an international trade association that governs and facilitates the exchange of information between member bureaus. These and other credit bureaus generally receive monthly or quarterly consumer accounts receivable data on computer tape from their subscribers or increasingly "talk" directly between computers via phone linkups. All these tapes are merged with existing records, or if none exists, a new file is created.

WHO REPORTS AND WHO DOESN'T

Virtually every commercial bank reports its consumer installment loans to one or more credit bureaus. Many savings banks and certain large savings and loan associations also report their loans. Also, banks often report the activity of their credit card holders (VISA, MasterCard or their own name brand). Many other credit cards also report. (American Express charge card does not report its accounts payment performance but it does subscribe to credit bureaus to check on an applicant's credit profile.) Most regional and national department stores—Sears Roebuck, J.C. Penney, Bloomingdale's, Macy's, Marshall Field, Bullock's, Saks Fifth Avenue, to name just a handful—account for much of the credit bureau's files.

Some of the businesses that do not report to credit bureaus are electric utilities, emergency rooms, most oil company credit card accounts, and Ma Bell. Many loans from colleges are not reported. Probably the biggest relief I supply to people all across the country when talking about credit bureaus is that the condition of your checking account is not reported to any bureau. People applaud upon learning that their record for bouncing checks stays within the bank and their own heads. (But keep in mind that banks will have a long memory.)

We have mentioned that your computerized credit bureau profile is now the single most important document besides your application that most credit granting institutions look at. Still, a great deal of smaller credit granting companies verify and screen your application in other ways and avoid the cost of receiving these credit bureau consumer profiles. And most of these companies, both large and small, do *not,* in fact, report the monthly activity of their customers to any credit bureau—at least not yet.

So there are really a variety of possible credit relationships or activities a company chooses to operate by. First, there are the businesses that neither ask for a credit bureau report nor give your subsequent record of repayment to anyone else. These are typically individual retailers and small family-owned and -operated chain stores, plus utilities, many gas credit cards, and colleges making loans. Virtually every company has at least an internal deadbeat or delinquent list of previous customers so that it can disqualify potential repeat offenders immediately.

Second, there are credit grantors who do not receive profiles per se but do screen out problem accounts to some degree by running their internally approved list of new customers through some sort of pooled list of delinquent or no-pay accounts in a central, industry-related credit bureau. The Direct Marketing Mail Association compiles such a list from its many members and will "prescreen" a mailing list before it is sent out. Hooper Holmes, based in Basking Ridge, New York, is one of the largest credit bureaus for the direct marketing industry, which includes mail order catalogues, publishing, record, and book clubs, toll-free telephone marketing via all media, and so on. They engage in prescreening and/or postscreening of their customers' lists based on delinquent account information provided them by these customers. The five largest consumer catalogue companies in the United States—Sears Roebuck, J.C. Penney, Montgomery Ward, Spiegel, and Aldens—all have extensive in-house credit departments and their own point systems to screen all credit orders. Through direct marketing and credit cards primarily, a huge number of nonfinancial businesses have created credit subsidiaries. Sears Roebuck is a prime example. At first simply a department store with a large and profitable catalogue business, Sears Roebuck has become transformed into a giant diversified financial services company by extending into multiline insurance (Allstate), real estate (Coldwell Banker), securities (Dean Witter Reynolds), and moneylending itself. Presumably, the credit records from each subsidiary will be available as marketing and credit tools for their total operation.

Another credit practice involves checking the credit bureau profile (or lack thereof) before accepting your application for their credit, but then declining to report to any agency the performance of their customers. Many banks do this with mortgage loans, and American Express currently operates in this fashion.

Still other credit grantors regularly receive and report to the credit bureau files on all potential and current customers. Department store and bank charge cards are their most faithful clients. Finally, some industries or individual companies receive from, or report to, credit bureaus only a portion of their accounts.

One type of credit granting company is not necessarily more valuable or dangerous to you than another; your consumer imperative, however, is to know the normal operational mode of any potential creditor and, more critically, to understand how you can involve yourself and change them where need be.

YOUR RIGHT TO SEE YOUR CREDIT FILE

The easiest way to track down which of the 1,900 credit bureaus contain data on you in their archives is to call up the department store where you have a charge account and ask the customer relations officer which credit reporting agency(ies) they subscribe to. (See the geographic credit bureau directory in Appendix C.) Also, ask your bank and insurance company which bureaus they use. The local Yellow Pages should list the firms in your area under "Credit Reporting Agencies" or "Credit Bureaus." In areas with separate consumer and business editions, credit bureaus sometimes hide out in the business Yellow Pages alone.

Equipped with this information, you can call or write to the proper credit bureau to ask for your report. Include your full name, address, social security number, and marital status. If you have been denied credit due to information contained within a credit bureau's files within the last 30 days, or have been notified of increases in interest or charges for credit or insurance due to adverse credit information, or if a debt collection agency notifies you that your credit rating may or has been adversely affected, you have the right by federal law to obtain the nature and substance of your credit report *without charge*. In all other instances, the credit bureau can impose a "reasonable charge" (currently ranging from $5 to $12). The agency must tell you the fee before giving you the information.

Many credit reporting agencies today welcome your involvement in inspecting, verifying, and elaborating on your credit report. They recognize the fact that the more accurate and complete their files are, the more useful tools they become to their credit granting customers who are charged on a per-request basis. TRW spends more than $4 million on consumer relations annually to explain its function. "We would be ecstatic if every adult knew about and exercised his rights," says Delia Fernandez, consumer sales manager of the Information Services Division of TRW Inc. Of the more than 35 million credit profiles sold in 1980 by TRW, only 500,000 consumers requested copies—and of those, fewer than 150,000 disputed their files' contents.

Not to be outdone, John L. Spafford, president of Associated Credit Bureaus, Inc., the international trade association of credit bureaus and the debt collection industry, says, "Credit bureaus are acutely aware of their responsibilities in maintaining the accuracy and privacy of consumer credit records. In effect, a credit record is an inventory of a consumer's bill-paying habits. It's a matter of policy for our trade association members and a matter of federal law as well that credit bureaus provide reasonable systems for proper access of credit data by legitimate credit grantors; that credit grantors who furnish the data to the bureau provide the most updated and accurate information; and that bureaus provide consumers with reasonable privacy safeguards and proper access to these records so the records can be updated or corrected when necessary."

Notwithstanding all of this industry cooperation, the Fair Credit Reporting Act of 1970 guarantees you a wide range of rights as a consumer while regulating the credit reporting agency business. Still, some credit bureaus may unwittingly fail to follow the provisions of this federal law or other state laws since enacted to expand your rights further. Make sure you are familiar with the following laws and firmly and responsibly insist that they are performed to your satisfaction.

In New York State, for example, you have the right to personally inspect your file for any reason at the credit bureau's office during normal business hours and be provided with trained personnel to explain any information in your report that is in code or trade terminology. In the course of preparing this book, we had to cite New York State's General Business Law before one national credit bureau doing business in New York would agree to let us stop by. Make sure you bring a driver's license or other certifiable identification to the appointment and enough money to pay for the report. You can take along one other person to the inspection.

The Fair Credit Reporting Act regulates all interstate credit bureaus, and applies to almost all of them, according to the Federal Trade Commission. Under this law, you have the right to be told—in detail—"the nature and substance" of your credit file. By specifying "nature and substance," Congress wanted to make sure that credit bureaus disclosed more than a mere summary of your credit profile. The specific status that you have with department stores and bank credit cards and so forth should be part of the record you receive. Medical information about you can still be withheld, however, much to the chagrin of lobbying consumer groups. While the federal law does not give you the right to see your actual file, many credit bureaus will supply it to you anyway. At the time the law was written, the credit bureau industry successfully lobbied that providing a hard copy of your file would prove too difficult for smaller credit bureaus to process mechanically. Since then, the rise of low-cost computerization and photocopying eliminated that excuse. Other states with fair credit reporting laws besides New York include Arizona, California, Connecticut, Kansas, Kentucky, Maine, Maryland, Massachusetts, Montana, New Hampshire, New Mexico, Oklahoma, and Texas.

When you request a copy of your credit report, also ask for a list of people or institutions that have received copies

of your report. FCRA gives you the right to know which
creditors have received the report *during the last six
months*. If your report was issued for employment purposes, you are entitled to know who has requested it in *the
last two years*.

READING YOUR CREDIT REPORT

Along with your credit report, you must receive by law a
written explanation of any codes or trade terminology used
in your file. Still, these profiles are prepared for credit
grantors—not for you, the consumer—and are often vex-
ingly oblique documents, needing further clarification.
Many negative inferences are made by creditors when interpreting this seemingly innocuous data. And various
credit bureaus package their reports in different forms (see
examples), but be patient and wade through it. It is important for you to understand exactly the following information that is recorded:

Account Profile.   Characterizes your overall status with
each credit grantor and court actions that you have been in
or are currently involved in. Credit bureaus have slightly
different styles, falling into two major categories. TRW employs a POS/NON/NEG mode. POS, or "positive," means
that your account is current, you've paid all your bills on
time or before 60 days. NON means "nonevaluated,"
which is supposedly a neutral rating for accounts that are 60
days late or more, but less than 90 days. The NON rating is
also given to inquiries (see explanation below) and accounts that have been delinquent for 60 days or more at a
time during the last three years but that are not current.
NEG obviously means "negative," a rating reserved for
those who are 90 days late or more on their payment for
that account. Bankruptcies, charge-offs, judgments settled,
and many other situations fall under the negative rating.
While TRW claims that the activity of its business cus-

tomers' accounts—or trade lines, as they are called within the business—is automatically designated under one of these categories as it is computed, we found several instances, while researching this book, in which credit grantors have adopted and printed their own credit interpretation. For instance, one New Jersey department store insists on giving nonevaluated ratings for a payment history with only one instance in the last twelve months of paying 30 days late. Another bank routinely issues a negative rating for falling behind on two monthly payments and subsequently catching up and even being ahead in repayment.

Most other credit bureaus connected with ACB, including Trans Union, Pinger, and Chilton, have for many years used a 1 through 9 rating system to grade each account, with 1 meaning "pays bills on time consistently" to 7, 8, and 9, which are various states of bankruptcy and default.* More and more, these credit bureaus are backing off from any overall status designation, and are willing to let the payment profile portion of the credit report speak for itself. Still, certain credit grantors are comfortable with the older 1 through 9 form, so you are apt to see it in your report, especially from one of the many smaller, local credit bureaus.

Your banker—or, more likely, a bank clerk—will scan down this column first to get a general impression of your standing with other creditors. If he or she sees too many negative and nonevaluated ratings (sometimes one negative account is too many), you will not get the loan.

Status/Comment. Provides a more detailed characterization of your repayment record. Again, the credit grantor is making the statement, not the credit bureau. The abbreviated notations, which are usually translated on the back of the form, generally refer to how long it took you to pay your bills in the past. A wide range of terse comments can become a part of this section of your credit profile—TRW

---

*The New York Telephone Company has a 1-5 credit score.

includes 84 kinds of status comments ranging from
"CURWAS30+6," which means "current account was 30
days past due six times or more," to "REDMD REPO,"
which translates to "account was a repossession now re-
deemed." Of the 84 comments TRW makes available to its
subscribers, only 10 are not negative in nature, if you include the "DECEASED" comment.

An "INQUIRY" notation on your profile signals that a
credit grantor has requested a copy of your credit profile.
When an inquiry line is not immediately followed by the
extension of credit, other potential credit grantors generally
assume it to mean that you were rejected for credit—
whether or not this, in fact, was the true course of events.
Often, credit grantors routinely pull a sample of their accounts merely to get a profile of their customers. These and
other incidents that create a solitary inquiry tradeline can
create a falsely damaging impression of your credit history
in the eyes of credit grantors who give your profile a curso-
ry inspection. These inquiries can remain in your file for up
to three years.

Subscriber Type/Association and Code/Terms. This logs
the credit grantor's account number for the credit bureau,
the type of account the creditor is making to you—"AUT"
means auto loan; "SEC" means a secured loan, or one in
which you provide collateral; "EDU" means an educational loan; and so forth. Association codes peg you to a specific contractual relationship to your creditor and state
whether it is a past or present event. The code sheet that
must be supplied to you will detail what the number or letter means—a past joint account with contractual responsibility, a simple individual account, and so on. Terms are
usually either quantified according to how many months
you have to repay or, in the case of certain charge cards, by
printing "REV," short for a revolving line of credit.

Amount and Balance. Self-explanatory, really, unless
your department store has not acknowledged recent pay-

ments, or there is some other clerical error that misstates the facts. The important aspect here is that a credit grantor will look at how much you are committed to repaying or how much you are allowed to borrow versus your income and the amount he is considering giving you credit for. If there is a lot of unused potential borrowing, it could be looked at in the same light as if you had or are about to borrow against it.

Balance Date. When the rest of the money is owed. Bankers and other credit grantors look for corresponding due dates for signs of possible trouble dealing with "balloon payments" (see Glossary).

Amount Past Due. How much you are behind in your payments. Again, check against your records.

Payment Profile. A form that is replacing the account profile as an objective measure of a consumer's payment pattern. With reference to monthly billings, the payment profile lists a "C" for every monthly payment on time or current. Numbers, meanwhile, signify how many days past due you paid the bill for a particular period. A damaging payment profile is often eliminated by adjusting a creditor's billing cycle to be in sync with yours.

In general, you should examine your credit profile closely to make sure that everything is in order, including your name, address, and spouse's name, and that all the account names are spelled correctly. Also, check your social security number(s), and all of the balances against your records.

MISTAKES IN YOUR CREDIT PROFILE

Credit bureaus process billions of bits of data. In this sophisticated process of constantly transferring information between machine and machine, people and machine, and people with people, mistakes are inevitable. Widespread name coincidence and similarities, misspellings, faulty

communication, and all sorts of bizarre human circumstances further compound the chances that you may find
patently false entries in your credit report. These mistakes
occur even though credit bureaus usually follow reasonable
procedures as required by law. In an environment where
low-level clerks have piped-in pop music or radios playing
beside their keyboard terminals while inputting your credit
information, mistakes can and do take place. Let's suppose
that of the 200 million consumer profiles generated annually there are, conservatively, 50 facts on each form. That's
10 billion facts or bits of information. If we assume a 1 percent margin of error, this means there can easily be 100
million mistakes in our nation's credit files, or a 50 percent
chance that you have an error on your credit profile.

Horror stories are legion. One middle-aged man told us
that he discovered in his report a trade line from Brooklyn
Savings Bank for a $5,000 loan. He had never dealt with
this bank in his life. The credit bureau's response: "Oh,
we've been getting a lot of those lately. The problem is that
Citibank's business I.D. (identification code number) is two
numbers away from Brooklyn Savings. We'll fix that right
away." Three weeks later, he received an updated copy of
his report, which showed the Brooklyn Savings trade line
indeed had been changed to his Citibank account. Unfortunately, four lines down on his report was another $5,000
loan from Citibank—the same transaction was listed twice
because his account number was transposed in part. Would
a banker who received this credit report have caught this
duplication and discounted one of the loans? "Certainly,
but that's not the way it's done today," responds a senior
lending officer at a major commercial bank. "Normally, a
banker would not get involved until the loan application has
already been rejected. On the appellate level, a banker
would catch it, but a clerk is reading the profile to add it up,
not to comprehend it per se."

The authoritative look of the physical document, with its
codes and computer type, makes the credit report an im-

posing presence. Another consumer related that he was "stunned and depressed" upon receiving his credit profile. "I always thought I had a good credit rating. I always paid my bills on time. But when I got the report, I just assumed I was guilty of these things." As a retired fireman from New Jersey, he had the time and the initiative (after some prodding) to visit personally with TRW and Trans Union. His admitted awe for authority suffered when he first noticed that TRW did not have any record of his VISA card account while Trans Union did, despite the fact that TRW insisted that VISA reported to them as well. Four months and five other mistakes later (it took seven updates of his TRW and Trans Union to finally fix these mistakes) he had lost his confidence in people's mastery over the machine. "They will swear up and down on the integrity of their information. But when you supply them with proof [of their error] and validate it, then they blame the computer."

Despite the credit bureaus' claims that their reports are objective, in practice these POS/NON/NEG and 1 through 9 rating systems are subjective systems that are inherently unfair. They are systems stacked against you because they do not deal with facts, but merely the representation of what its subscribers claim. These "facts" can be totally wrong or disputed by you. Moreover, they do not allow for an explanation of your actions.

Another problem with credit bureaus is their long-standing predilection for ferreting out and emphasizing the negative aspects of your credit history. They believe that their paying customers—your potential credit grantors—are more interested in knowing about the one time you slipped rather than the long list of times you performed well and proved your creditworthiness. Too often, a piece of negative information continues to hound you long after you have resolved the problem to the satisfaction of the credit grantor. A very small account at Stern's department store is listed as nonevaluated by TRW because the charge customer missed one monthly payment of $10. Despite TRW's public interpretation that an account is not bumped from the "positive status" until at least one bill has gone to 60 days, Stern's own interpretation is in force when the account profile is downgraded.

What other potential credit grantors assume are facts are not necessarily facts, but what they demand as clients of the credit bureaus. The rudest injustice is that so much of this electronic reproduction of our supposed habits as billpayers and borrowers can be amassed without our knowledge or corroboration. A credit grantor's statement is not automatically a fact until it is verified by you, the consumer.

Your involvement in making and policing your credit profile is absolutely vital to maximizing your creditworthiness and freeing yourself of unseen reins.

GETTING INVOLVED

If, after carefully reviewing your credit report, you believe there are items that are erroneous, vague, or misleading, write a letter to the credit agency outlining your objections. Retain a copy for your files and bring a copy with you to the bank. The letter should forthrightly state that you want the credit bureau to investigate and delete the data that it cannot substantiate or that might be misinterpreted. The credit bureau is obliged by federal law to reinvestigate and correct or eliminate errors or ambiguities. Its failure to do so *in timely fashion* requires the agency to delete the entire entry from its computer file—whether it is true or false. Trans Union and TRW have established company policies of limiting the length of time to resolve errors or disputed matters to 15 working days; if they cannot obtain verification within that span of time, it is electronically expunged. Since the burden of proof shifts back to the credit bureaus for once, do not be timid about challenging what you feel is unjustly derogatory information.

Your credit agency, however, is protected from a wholesale repudiation of its records by being allowed to consider disputes "frivolous or irrelevant." Your letter is less apt to fall into the "frivolous" category if you avoid rambling on about incidental matters making accusatory diatribes. State your case succinctly and enclose any pertinent copies of corroborative material if it is available. Keep a copy for your files.

Sample Letter of Dispute

Dear Sirs:

I have found the following errors in my credit report and would like them corrected forthwith:

(Error Listing)

I have contacted the credit grantors and they are awaiting your call.

Sincerely,

Terminology like "Delinquent," "Judgment satisfied," "Discharged in bankruptcy," "Defaulted," or "Charged off" carries the tone of harsh condemnation. If you can establish a legitimate reason for your slow pay and document it, you should press for the correction or elimination of the dereliction. Often, you can correct the report by paying the bill, or catching up in payments. A consumer with a loan from Chase Manhattan who missed only one month's payment was understandably furious when he found himself listed as a *negative account* on his TRW. He made an appointment with the loan officer in charge and, showing the banker his report, said, "What is my incentive to pay you back in timely fashion on the remainder of the loan if you have given me this negative rating?" He left the office with a letter from Chase instructing TRW to change his status to nonevaluated and eliminate any mention of delinquencies. The "facts" can be changed despite the official protestations of the credit bureaus.

FIXING THE PROBLEM CREDIT BUREAU PROFILE

The very use of the term "fact" with regard to the credit bureaus and their customers, the credit grantors, are not as we know it in the biblical sense. Facts are often perceptions. Facts can be edited. Facts can be modified. The following conversation with a credit-poor client demonstrates what can and has been done:

"Last summer I had been unable to get any new credit for various reasons: I had two negative items in my credit file (MasterCard and VISA with two different banks canceled about two years before for three consecutive months of nonpayment), only one positive item (a current department store account), and apparent job instability (I had been working as a consultant engineer with several client companies each year; it appeared on the credit bureau profiles, however, that I couldn't hold a job).

"I had been paying small amounts each month according to agreements reached with MasterCard and VISA in the vain hope that this would demonstrate my creditworthiness; that my accounts would then be reinstated; and that the black marks would be removed magically from my file. During this time, however, high interest rates and state usury laws made the bank credit card business unattractive for banks and my accounts were not reinstated for one excuse or another.

"At the time I heard your lecture, the laws had finally been changed and rates were beginning to fall. Following your advice, I made my move.

"First, I got copies of my TRW and Trans Union files and corrected all trivial errors (address, employer, etc.).

"Second, I called my MasterCard bank in Boston and agreed to pay my entire balance (approximately $400) if he would have the negative item removed by TRW and Trans Union. He did, I did, and they did. I requested copies of my file to make sure they did!

"On all of my recent applications I put one of my current client engineering companies as my employer since 1977.

This is technically true since I have worked for them off and on since then, I am doing work for them now, and (most importantly) their personnel department will back me up.

"People seem to think telling the truth means sharing your whole life story to some credit clerk who reads these things. One woman who has a long association teaching art in the evenings at a major New York university has been putting 'free-lance artist' on her applications because that's how she thinks of herself! Of course, she has gotten nowhere. I told her to write 'teacher,' which is filling out her application correctly without lying.

"Next, I opened a MasterCard account with a Virginia savings and loan that is completely secured by *my* money in a savings account. Effectively, when I use my card, I'm borrowing from myself and paying the bank interest plus $25 a year for the privilege. It is, however, a valid MasterCard and undistinguishable as a credit reference from any other bank card.

"I had an explanatory paragraph entered into my file at TRW and Trans Union regarding my VISA account. Trans Union put it in as I requested. TRW, amazingly, deleted the correct negative information regarding VISA instead of putting my statement on file. I was starting to get ahead of the game!

"I had applied and had been turned down recently for a Diners Club card. The reason they gave me was negative information in my credit file. I sent them a letter asking to be reconsidered and included an explanation of my history with VISA, photocopies of my VISA statements showing regular payments, and a brief sketch of my income and expenses demonstrating my ability to repay. *They sent me a card*.

"I reapplied to Chase VISA for reinstatement including all the above mentioned information as well (of course) as my new credit references and with *no mention* of the Boston account. They reinstated my account two months ago and cleared my TRW and Trans Union file. (I checked, and had my consumer statement removed.)

"Two department stores that I normally would not do business with have this month sent me credit cards without my requesting them. Of course, I'll take them and use them once in awhile for socks or something.

"The result to date is that my file now shows five positive items of consumer credit and no negative items. It took a bit of doing but I finally feel free."

ADDING A CONSUMER STATEMENT

If you believe that the credit agency has not responded adequately to your first letter by changing or deleting contested portions of your credit profile, you are entitled by law to submit a statement explaining these delinquencies and any other problems. Although this can be of any length, credit agencies have the right to limit you to 100 words. If they do so, they will help you in the preparation and editing.

Here's your chance to balance the often negative information in your credit file with positive data. Your letter should be truthful, forthright, positive. It should set forth the extraordinary events that might explain any judgment, tax lien, or attachments. This explanation may go a long way to mitigate the negative disposition of your potential credit grantor.

Here's a sample consumer statement for an applicant with many problems—slow payment, a judgment against him, and so on:

Dear Sirs:

With reference to your credit report on me, I would like to record the following facts explaining items that appear *to be negative.*

1. The Macy's judgment for $1,500 was levied after my estranged wife purchased merchandise in a buying *spree following our separation. For some time now my lawyer has been trying to straighten the matter out.*

2. I incurred a slow payment record in 1976 because of a bout with hepatitis that resulted in a temporary cash shortage. Despite this income difficulty, all back payments were ultimately met.

3. The IRS tax lien as recorded by you took me completely by surprise. I have no knowledge of its origin, and I have instructed my accountant to make a searching inquiry into the matter. I shall immediately inform you of the results.

Sincerely,

This consumer statement then becomes an integral part of your credit profile. Insist that it be *included* in the reports on you sent out by the credit bureau (and not merely referred to on the profile as being present in some backup file). You should also request in a cover letter to the credit reporting agency that you want your updated credit profile, including your consumer statement, to be mailed to everyone who denied you credit based on the old credit report.

Appended to a rather checkered credit bureau report, the following consumer statement impressed us with its forthrightness and concern:

"In the past I have experienced numerous problems— illness, divorce. At this time, I have reached a point in my life where I would like to correct all mistakes made prior to the date of this entry. I would appreciate if you would start judging my creditworthiness from this date on. There is no reason why I should ever be delinquent on any account again."

STARTING FROM SCRATCH: CREDIT REVISIONS
If you have no credit record, you have no credit. Hundreds of thousands of Americans are denied credit each

year precisely because their credit experience has not been chronicled by a credit bureau.

Perhaps the most significant way to improve your credit profile—or create one out of nothing—is to add positive information that the credit bureau does not normally incorporate. A majority of the 1,900 credit bureaus, in an effort to fill out their inventories, will agree to input other credit information *at the consumer's request.* Just because one or more of your creditors does not normally report your fine payment record to a credit bureau file that will be scanned before you are approved for a loan does not prohibit you from intervening to make this information more generally known. You can, for example, benefit from your prompt payment of your phone and electric bills and excellent internal rating there by requesting the release of your credit record to you in writing. In many parts of the country, if you indicate that you need to start a file with a credit bureau in order to qualify for credit, many otherwise nonreporting credit grantors stated to us that their credit department will release to you their rating.

Most credit bureaus, including Trans Union, will then agree to enter this positive credit information into your files once you supply them with the written authorization and proof, for a slight fee (currently, $1.50 per entry or "tradeline").

By identifying positive nonreporting current or recent credit experiences, and upgrading the relationships to official credit references, you can establish your credit profile where none existed or help to balance an otherwise spotty record with more notice of good credit performance. Consider any relationships with small independent businesses like hardware or jewelry stores, oil company credit cards, college loans that often go unreported, loans from family or friends, or even your record of tithing or other regular contributions based on an agreement with an eleemosynary institution.

The trick here is that you are entitled to get the benefit of the good information from both personal and mechanized credit sources.

Again, before you fill out any application for credit, check with the major consumer credit bureaus in your area for a copy of your files. Remember, to get a free look at your file, you have to have been denied credit by a reporting creditor within the last 30 days or have had a collection agency threaten to report your alleged delinquency. Otherwise, you will generally be charged between $5 and $10 at current rates for a copy of your profile.

In this process, many credit bureaus will want to know who specifically denied you credit. While they maintain that this provision is merely part of their verification process, designed to prevent anyone and everyone from receiving free files at their expense, complying with them could hurt you unnecessarily. When you are denied credit, you must be told in writing if this denial was based on information received from a credit profile and, if so, which credit bureau. However, a number of creditors report to more than one credit bureau and, further, credit bureaus often exchange information received from different clients. Often, therefore, you have no way of knowing if another credit bureau has been supplied with the fact that you have been denied credit. Volunteering this information is tantamount to giving them valuable negative data that may not have found its way into your profile otherwise.

You should refuse to supply specifics beyond the generic type of institution involved (department store, charge card, etc.), unless you are certain that your denial has already been reported to that credit bureau. Some credit bureaus might still resist, claiming that they have no legal requirement to provide you with a free summary unless it was based upon information in their file. Rather than risk the damage of adding a negative tradeline to your profile, pay the fee for your file. But get even. Send a written complaint about their anticonsumer bias to the Federal Trade Commission, Credit Practices (address in Appendix B, "Where to Push the Up Button"), with copies to your local state and congressional representatives. If enough people complain, your state, the FTC, or Congress might amend the law to require the credit bureau industry to send out free profiles annually to anyone who requests it in writing. After all, our names are their valuable inventory, and because they are making money from our private financial dealings, we should have it shown to us periodically as part of a consumer verification process.

YOUR ANNUAL CREDIT CHECKUP

Otherwise creditworthy people often run into problems because they discover gross errors or deletions from their credit history in their credit report in the midst of or after being denied an important request for credit. When I was lecturing at Yale, a professor told me that he was initially turned down for a mortgage because his credit record had not been transferred from Des Moines, Iowa. He hadn't thought of it. As much as credit bureaus like to think otherwise, you cannot assume that your credit history is in itself portable. You have to take care to transport it along with your other belongings.

Due to the emerging enormity of the credit bureau profile in America as the contemporary arbiter of our respectability and our good names, we strongly recommend that you make at least an annual review of your credit profile for its accuracy and completeness. It is a small price to pay for protecting and maximizing your credit credentials.

Chapter Three

The Secret World of Scoring

Have you ever wondered where the credit grantors of America found the time and personnel to examine the millions of applications submitted to them every year?

The answer is, they don't, because there is no time and not enough personnel—so they "score." That is, they use a system of "credit scoring," which rates applications according to a point system, rather than using the human judgments of a credit officer.

Almost every major lender or credit grantor scores you in some way: banks like Citibank, Chase Manhattan, and Bank of America; department stores like Sears Roebuck, Bullock's, and Montgomery Ward; charge card companies like Diners Club; most finance companies; even the phone company. Everybody does it but no one is eager to talk about it. While researching an article on consumer borrowing for *New York* magazine, we found that nearly every major bank refused to confirm the widespread use of credit scoring. And yet, when we printed that scoring was, in fact, a prevalent practice according to our findings, there was no word of objection or denial.

The reason for the scoring "craze" today is simple—money. Scoring saves money for the big, high-volume credit grantors in two basic ways: (1) It dramatically reduces overhead and payroll previously allocated to credit approvers (one lender proudly reported recently that it was able to make decisions in 50,000 to 60,000 applications a month using just five clerks in lieu of a staff of credit approvers). (2) It cuts down delinquencies, collection expenses, and charge-offs by more accurately predicting better credit risks—purely in terms of a system of statistical odds.

Nevertheless, in spite of all the praises sung to scoring in the financial trade journals, there has been little public disclosure of the existence of scoring systems or how they work. Scoring has been shrouded in secrecy. Credit grantors are wary of revealing too much information about the characteristics of their scoring systems because, they say, they're concerned that applicants might be tempted to lie about the facts in order to reach the right score. Some lenders are even cautious in their rejection letters—they mask the characteristics of their scoring systems by listing a large number of possible reject reasons, including legally prohibited ones (which are never checked), and then checking only the ones that are appropriate.

Both users and creators of credit scoring systems are extremely sensitive about publicity these days, especially since a number of consumer credit organizations have criticized the fairness of scoring systems. These systems might be "empirically derived and statistically sound," but they are unintentionally biased against women, sometimes minorities, credit neophytes, and other potential good credit risks who just don't happen to fit the "credit-clone" of a scoring system.

While scoring is a useful tool for credit grantors, it is part of an invisible, secret world that obscures the true credit process. To know about scoring is not to defraud it, but to understand it, like the credit bureau profile, and to confront it when it does not reflect the strengths of your creditworthiness. You have to know the score before you can even it.

THE STATISTICS OF SCORING

Most scoring systems are designed by one of several companies that specialize in credit scoring systems: Fair, Isaac and Co. (San Rafael, Calif.); General Electric Credit Corp. (Stamford, Conn.); Mathtech (Princeton, N.J.); the Richards and Sparks Company (Richmond, Va.); Management Decision Systems (Atlanta, Ga.); Credit Management Association (Worthington, Ohio); and Robert Cliff & Associates (Alameda, Calif.)—to name a few of the better known scoring designers. Generally, one of these companies is approached by a bank or other credit grantor to tailor a scoring system to its particular pool of applicants. These scoring systems are expensive, so in order for them to be cost-effective, a credit grantor usually has to take in at least 1,000 applicants a month or band together with other credit grantors to develop a larger pool of data.

The scoring system designer begins with a pool of the lender's past applicants—say, 4,500 applicants, equally divided among 1,500 satisfactory files, 1,500 rejects, and 1,500 seriously delinquent or charge-off accounts. The designer then analyzes the answers to each question to determine which questions are the best indicators of "creditworthiness"—whether the loans or credit extensions were paid back. Out of 60 to 90 questions on an application, 6 to 10 usually prove to be leading indicators of credit performance. These questions are weighted according to their importance in predicting payers versus nonpayers, and the range of potential answers are then assigned various point values. Finally, the scoring system designer calculates a total cutoff score to meet the instructions of the lender. For example, if a lender wants to keep his delinquency rate under 2 percent, the point cutoff might be set at 280 points;

that is, if the lender only accepted people who scored 280 points or higher, the statistical odds are that these accept-ances would result in no more than 2 percent bad debt.

ADDING UP YOUR SCORE

Let's look at an example of a hypothetical scoring sheet for a bank loan application (see T-1). The sheet shows that the applicant, Sydney Carton, was scored according to sev-en key indicators on his application: (1) years at home ad-dress; (2) living facilities (own/rent); (3) bank references; (4) years on job; (5) department store/charge/credit cards; (6) age of his automobile; and (7) number of home tele-phones. Since Sydney has lived at his current address for three and a half years, he scored 34 points; he rents an un-furnished apartment (38 points); he has both a checking and savings account at Tillson's (63 points); he has been em-ployed at the same job for three and a half years (38 points); he has both a department store and a major charge card (56 points); his car is three years old (38 points); and he has one phone (25 points). So far, Sydney has scored 292 points on his application, but his credit history with the bank is a little shaky—he had some financial difficulties two years ago and was late in making several monthly payments toward the car loan he had taken out with his bank (−20 points). His other credit history is satisfactory, though, with no de-rogatory information and just one inquiry made by a de-partment store to which he is applying for a credit card (18 and 3 points).

If the cutoff were indeed 280 points, Sydney, with 293 points, would have made it. In some banks, however, there is a "gray area" (often 20 points above the cutoff and 20 points below) where the credit officer in charge can over-ride the score, using his or her own judgment of the appli-cant's creditworthiness (note the space at the bottom of the score sheet marked "Override Authorized by _____"). Naturally, the designers of credit scoring systems hate it when their clients override the scores with human judgment: it "ruins" the test of their design. They cite examples like Sears Roebuck, which reportedly found that in 95 percent of the cases where their credit managers overrode a "no" of the scoring system, the loans were difficult or impossible to collect.

Because scoring systems are designed for particular companies and applicant pools, the key questions that are scored in each case might vary widely. Frequently, people are scored on occupation, length of time at their current job and home address, number of department store charge cards and other credit cards, income and debt-to-income ratio (the amount of your monthly debt in comparison to monthly income), finance company references, home phone, age of auto, and age of applicant (although this may be tricky, since it is illegal to discriminate against the elderly).

The Federal Housing Administration, in evaluating mortgage applications, scores such characteristics as "motivating interest in ownership of the property," "adequacy of available assets for transaction," and "stability of effective income." And companies in the direct marketing field often use scoring systems that reflect the unique nature of the industry. In their own literature, the Direct Mail Marketing Association relates that many direct mail marketers assign points depending upon type of item ordered (the customer ordering Beethoven's symphonies is a better bet than the one ordering *The Best of Led Zeppelin*); type of address (e.g., P.O. Box or General Delivery is considered a sign of poor risk); writing instruments used (a pen with blue or black ink is desirable whereas pencil or red ink is symptomatic of a problem order); and general geographic region (big cities are notorious for producing big collection problems).

In many cases, we have no idea why certain indicators "work"; the scoring system is simply concerned with probability, the odds that an applicant will pay back. Nevertheless, the scorer's method of "discriminant analysis" generally focuses on characteristics that claim to demonstrate

SAMPLE SCORE SHEET

TILLSON'S BANK

Date:	
Account #:	964732-51-8990
Applicant:	Sydney Carton
Scored by:	E. B. Lorry

BASE SCORE APPLICATION

							SCORE
YEARS AT HOME ADDRESS	Less than 6 mos. 15	6 mos. to 2 yrs. 5 mos. 25	2½ yrs. to 6 yrs. 5 mos. 34	6½ yrs. to 10 yrs. 5 mos. 40	10½ yrs. & over 50		34
OWN/RENT	Own/Buying 56	Renting 38	Relative (Living w/ Parents) 30	Other (Trailer, Motel) 10			38
BANK REFERENCE	No Account 20	Savings 38	Checking 38	Both 63			63
YEARS ON JOB	Less than 6 mos. 10	6 mos. to 1 yr. 5 mos. 28	1½ yrs. to 2 yrs. 5 mos. 32	2½ yrs. to 5 yrs. 5 mos. 38	5½ yrs. to 12 yrs. 5 mos. 42	12½ yrs. & over 45	38
DEPT. STORE CHARGE/CREDIT CARDS	None 0	Dept. Store 22	Major Credit/ Charge Card 35	Both 56			56
AGE OF AUTO	No Auto 20	1–2 yrs. 42	3 yrs. 38	4–5 yrs. 33	5 yrs. & over 28		38

HOME TELEPHONE

No Phone	One	Two	Three		
0	25	36	42	25	SUBTOTAL 292

IN-HOUSE RECORDS

	Satisfactory	No Record	New Customer	Major/Minor Derog.		
MOST RECENT RATING	12	7	7	−20	−20	SUBTOTAL 272

CREDIT BUREAU

	None	No Record	One	Two	Three	
MAJOR/MINOR DEROG.	18	7	−2	−10	−30	18

	No Record	No Inquiries	One	Two	Three		
# INQUIRIES OR TOO NEW TO RATE	12	12	3	−6	−22	3	TOTAL 293

OVERRIDE AUTHORIZED BY _____

43

"stability." For example, those attributes that indicate a borrower has put down "roots" in his or her community—there is a long tenure at the same job and in the same home, and there is a home phone (bad credit risks usually don't have one). Occupation is sometimes an indication of stability, with more points going to professionals and the fewest points to unskilled workers. However, Sears Roebuck has found that occupation offers no predictive value of credit-worthiness and some banks have found that lawyers and doctors are chronically late payers. Furthermore, lifelong laborers might score higher than neophytes in white-collar jobs, and the self-employed, whatever the occupation, are suspect.

Income, as a stability indicator, is important not only in how much is earned (more is generally better), but in how much an applicant has to spare each month. One retailer, for example, found that in certain parts of the country the credit history of its customers got worse when incomes rose between $16,000 and $24,000. (More money may mean more obligations and less disposable income.) Similarly, age is usually an indicator of stability—the older a person is, the better, although scores tend to dip during the heavy spending years of consumer life (the thirties and forties).

As we showed on the hypothetical sheet, the applicant's credit history is extremely important. Even if you score well on the key indicators of your application, a poor credit history with your bank or other derogatory information on your credit bureau report will often negate a good score. Furthermore, as mentioned in Chapter 2, having no history on your credit profile does not help your case. No news is not good news, and you are ordinarily given a minimal score.

GEOGRAPHICAL SCORING

Most credit grantors that take applicants from all over the United States break down their scoring system into regions. These regional scoring systems generally divide the country into three to 30 segments. The divisions are carefully tailored, but not so specifically as to constitute "redlining"—scoring by neighborhoods is illegal, and Montgomery Ward was fined $175,000 several years ago by the Federal Trade Commission for scoring zip codes in determining whether to grant credit to its customers. What regional scoring does is "weight" certain credit characteristics to reflect the particular consumer behavior—the "psychographics"—of different parts of the country. In building five regional scoring systems for one of its clients, Fair, Isaac found that its regional systems were "one third more powerful" than scoring based on national averages—that is, regional scoring was one third more effective in reducing bad debt.

Scoring by geography produces some interesting twists and peculiarities in the typical scoring trends. One Fair, Isaac customer reported that income level was useful in distinguishing applicants from Chicago but of no help at all in dealing with those from Denver. Length of residence is apparently not a useful indicator in Iowa because people tend not to move—"people only move *out* of Iowa," quipped one scoring company executive.

Sears Roebuck has found that while homeowners are generally better credit risks than renters, the reverse is true in some parts of the country. In these cases, the occupants of mobile homes or rented quarters were apparently military officers who lived near their base, and these applicants tended to be more careful with their credit than local homeowners. The distinction between civilians and military employees sometimes produces differences in scoring length of employment: while a longer tenure at one job is usually a sign of stability; for a four-year military enlistee, less time is better. That is, he or she is more stable six months into the military term than three and one half years out, at which point there may be a change of lifestyle and earning power. The possible result of regional scoring, then, is that an army general living in Virginia could be scored like a graduate student if he moved to Boston.

THE PROLIFERATION OF SCORING

First considered as early as 1941, the practice of credit scoring went through two decades of sporadic experimentation, then grew dramatically during the 1970s, mainly through the research and development of several credit scoring design companies. Fair, Isaac, generally acknowledged as the industry leader, produced its first scoring system in 1959 and has designed 750 systems for various companies since then. General Electric Credit Corporation, which has been developing scoring systems since 1961, has produced systems for each of its own offices as well as for over 30 credit unions.

Today, Montgomery Ward (reported to have one of the most sophisticated systems in operation) uses credit scoring in all its stores. Sears Roebuck began scoring in 1968 and has extended it to more than a quarter of its regional credit card granting stores; and the Bank of America, with half a million credit card applicants a year, relies heavily on scoring. At least 16 of the 20 largest consumer finance companies currently use scoring systems, and many companies, large and small, are likely to follow suit during this decade. Very quietly, credit scoring has become as pervasive in the consumer credit industry as the credit bureau profile.

It's no accident that scoring has been heralded in many credit circles. Given a volatile interest rate environment, the institution of credit controls, and the boom in bankruptcies, credit grantors have looked to scoring as a means of reducing bad debt. David Sparks, of the scoring design company, Richards and Sparks, has called credit scoring "the fourth C of credit" and suggested to consumer bankers the notion of four Cs within credit scoring itself.

• *Control*. Scoring offers a means of regulating the number of loans or credit cards being granted; tightening up or loosening up credit can be accomplished simply by raising or lowering the cutoff score.

• *Consistency*. Scoring brings "consistent evaluations of all applicants, consistent assessment of lender performance, and consistent communication and application of credit policy."

• *Cost Benefits*. By "improving portfolio quality," scoring reduces bad debt without reducing the number of applicants. And by replacing credit officers with increasingly automated methods of application processing, scoring substantially reduces payroll and overhead. "Mature" systems virtually eliminate human involvement in the screening process, aside from the two minutes or so that it takes to type the data from an application into a computer terminal. Fair, Isaac proudly maintains that one of its systems typically will reduce credit investigation and charge-off expenses by at least 20 percent without considering other indirect savings such as reduced collection expenses.

• *Compliance*. Scoring has been effective in demonstrating credit grantors' compliance with federal law—specifically, the Equal Credit Opportunity Act (ECOA).

While credit scoring began long before Congress passed the Equal Credit Opportunity Act in 1974, the pressure of compliance to federal law has given unwitting benefits to scoring, sparking an awareness and enthusiasm among credit grantors that did not previously exist. ECOA prohibits discrimination in credit transactions based upon race, color, religion, national origin, sex, marital status, or receipt of public assistance—and credit scoring, based on statistical probability, has been turned to as an acceptable means of compliance.

Regulation B, written by the Federal Reserve Board to implement ECOA, does not require the use of scoring sys-

tems. It does, however, allow the use of systems that are
"demonstrably and statistically sound and empirically derived." These systems must be "based on a creditor's recent experience with credit applications and generally accepted statistical techniques must be used from sampling
and validation." This means, for example, that even though
ECOA prohibits discrimination based on age through judgmental analysis, it allows creditors to include age as a characteristic in a scoring system, provided that an applicant 62
years or older is not assigned a negative value for age
(many creditors have found that people over 70 actually
have the best credit record of any age group). Thus, credit
scoring has given credit grantors a means of discouraging
lawsuits that claim discrimination under systems of human
judgment.

THE SCORE OF SCORING

If scoring offers a "demonstrably and statistically
sound" credit evaluation system, what's wrong with it?

Everything, if credit grantors—especially banks—rely
exclusively on scoring to determine the creditworthiness of
applicants. Fair, Isaac's premise that "intuition is no match
for a good scoring system" may be necessary for large national credit grantors that cannot realistically meet with
millions of applicants. But where consumer lending is concerned, scoring systems by themselves are not enough;
there can be no substitute for personal evaluation, as time-
consuming as that might be. As one banker has told us:
"One thing a computer can't do is evaluate people. It can't
take the place of a human being."

While scoring systems make systematic, consistent judgments, they do not allow for creditworth exceptions. Like
all systems, they are liable to give short shrift to anyone
outside narrow norms. If you happen to exhibit a particular
characteristic of stability that a scoring system is not designed to measure, that value does not count. You, the ap-

plicant, are put in a position where you could "strike out" without even getting a chance to swing the bat.

Women, ironically, may be discriminated against by scoring systems that comply with ECOA regulations designed to protect women from credit discrimination. This particular situation arises because the law requires that applicants be scored without regard to sex. Placing women in the same applicant pool as men places them at a disadvantage since the characteristics of scoring systems are determined by male-dominated credit data—women are simply much newer to the credit game. Women generally score less than men because they have lower incomes, work at lower level jobs, own less real estate, and have less credit history. Nevertheless, this lower economic level does not accurately reflect the credit performance of women, according to a 1976 study conducted by professors Gary Chandler and David Ewart for the Credit Research Center at Purdue University. For example, Chandler and Ewart found that if men typically handled financial matters, only one or two bank references might be an indicator of risk, while for women, the establishment of even one such relationship was often indicative of a good credit performance. Owning a house showed much more creditworthiness in women than in men, while having a low income or a retail job was less of an indicator of "negatives" for women than for men.

When Chandler and Ewart developed scoring systems exclusively for women, they found that women would be granted more credit than in a system that pooled men and women together. "ECOA and Regulation B seem to be unduly concerned with form and not sufficiently concerned with performance," they concluded. "Females and males need not be subjected to the same set of rules if there is a rational basis for concluding that they are not similarly situated."

Scoring works against those who have not yet had a chance to demonstrate stability. It creates problems for those who have just moved into an area; indeed, it does not consider the reasons for moving, which in today's business world might indicate steady, consistent job advancement. It discriminates against younger people who have not yet had a chance to develop a credit history. While Fair, Isaac suggests that scoring lenders could benefit from using special questionnaires for applicants under 30 or 35, these designs must be careful not to discriminate against the elderly. Furthermore, scoring systems might inadvertently discriminate against minorities: one western banker quietly told us that her bank's scoring system found that a history with a finance company was indicative of poor creditworthiness—it just so happened that this type of credit behavior was prevalent among the area's black population.

Scoring also might be flawed in ways that are difficult to remedy because of the very methodology used to create the systems. As Robert Eisenbeis, a member of the Federal Reserve Board's research staff, reported some years ago, credit scoring models are usually based upon samples of loans that have been granted, rather than on potential borrowers or through-the-door applicants. Short of granting loans to all comers, the user of a scoring model must estimate the model with a "truncated population" of approved borrowers. By necessity, said Eisenbeis, this estimation process created unknown biases. In other words, the very pool upon which any model is based is inevitably skewed and self-limiting.

Finally, any scoring system is subject to a certain amount of error from the clerks who score applications: errors in transcription or simple addition; errors in interpreting the data and assigning the correct point value. Fair, Isaac has found that, depending upon the type of monitoring system used to insure consistency among scoring personnel, the amount of error among its client companies varied from 5 percent to 50 percent.

Although the technical and human problems of scoring are being reworked by scoring design companies, the larger

question about scoring remains: Why should a model of stability—which may not reflect *your* particular stability—potentially eliminate the "hearing" you deserve in order to
demonstrate your case? The elimination of this hearing is
fundamentally unfair and incompatible with our traditional
American ways.

Even if scoring truly reduces bad debt and hence the cost
of extending credit, *you* should not accept it at the expense
of losing your hearing. After all, scoring is still just a system
of statistical probability and you are not a statistic. Even if
you think you know how you will be scored, you should
"personalize" your application—remove it from the realm
of probability and bounce it to someone with discretion. As
we will explain more fully in the next chapter, you must
footnote the answers on your application to inhibit routine
scoring. This is not a scheme to beat the system. It is the
exercise of your right to make the system respond to you.

While banks, credit unions, and finance companies frequently exercise human judgment as well as score you, retailers and national credit and charge card issuers have
moved progressively toward straight scoring. Still, this
does not mean you cannot even the score. We know of one
recent instance in which a young woman was turned down
for a national charge card because she did not score well—
even though she had been working for a newspaper for
three years; earned $25,000 a year; had charge accounts at
Brooks Brothers and Bergdorf Goodman's; and never
bounced a check at her bank, Morgan Guaranty. After she
was informed in writing that she had scored "lowest" in
three areas (length of present employment, credit references, and type of occupation), she told her story to a fellow reporter who decided to call the public relations officer
of the charge card company to inquire about the case.
Shortly afterward, the PR officer called back to say that
"somehow the computer had made an error and a 'review
by humans' had made his friend deserving."

Scoring systems, however well designed, cannot be divorced from human judgments; they *reflect* human judgments carried out by computers. The acceptable cutoff score in any system is not a final statement on one's creditworthiness. A cutoff score may be affected by a bank's need to regulate its volume of loans at any particular time and, as such, it is as much a reflection of transient business needs as it is a judgment of your ability to pay back.

Bankers, especially, have an obligation to their communities—a social responsibility to say yes or no based, in part, upon a personal and qualitative relationship with their customers. Because the establishment of credit means so much more than the loan bankers must reorganize and exercise their role as lending officers. Credit scoring provides lenders with a useful guideline, but if they use scoring to replace their human function, then they are abdicating their most important responsibility.

Chapter Four

Choosing Your Banker: Creating the Power of Trust

THE SPECIFICS OF HOW YOU FILL OUT YOUR APPLICATION FOR credit are largely influenced by where you are applying. For the next couple of chapters, we are concentrating on the most difficult type of credit request: the unsecured consumer loan, typically the installment loan from a bank. Yet for all of the numerous kinds of loans that banks make available to certain of its customers, including VISA and MasterCard, an understanding of the people at the bank with whom you will be dealing is required.

Personalization—this is your key to every step of the borrowing process. Just as you must enter and correct the computerized world of credit profiles, understand the practice of credit scoring, and then fill out your loan application in a way that best presents your past and present abilities, you must prepare to meet with your banker and create an environment of trust. Before your loan application is complete, you should find a trusted banker in order to have that loan officer personally "shepherd" your application through the system.

When I was a loan officer, I saw far too many potential

borrowers timidly enter the bank without an appointment as if they were slipping into their first "open call" audition. They looked dazed and confused. While many good bankers will try to accommodate this "off-the-street" business, such insecurity and ignorance of the proper borrowing process creates more work for the banker, lowers his or her initial impression of you, and consequently greatly diminishes your chances of qualifying for a loan.

The simple solution to circumventing the gaffs of an impromptu screening lies in the planning. The bank you intend to get a loan from should be carefully selected and *stalked* in advance. By determining your best bet in a bank, arranging for a good introduction to that bank, and preparing yourself for a meeting with your banker, you will be creating an environment where your self-confidence and trust grow. In borrowing you can set your own stage, one where the "acoustics" bring out the best in you.

PICKING YOUR BANK

Just as corporations work at evaluating and developing ties to the lending institutions that best serve their needs, consumers should use their skills to choose and work with the banks that are best for them. There is no such thing as "The Banks"—a faceless, monolithic mass. Banks are simply people and exhibit the same attributes and idiosyncrasies as the rest of humanity. Because each bank employs its own people, different banks develop different corporate priorities, different "personalities." (Ironically, I had to emphasize this point that people make the difference to a new crop of bank trainees who expressed concern about how they were to compete in an environment where all the banks—and other businesses—provide basically the same services.)

Lending institutions do share one universal trait—they all want to maximize profits. When scouting for a bank to borrow from, it is useful therefore to think of yourself as the object of a bank's profit. Besides your confidence in your ability to repay your loan with interest, what else do you have to offer a bank? Certainly a checking account with a reasonable monthly balance and/or a passbook savings account are both very profitable to banks today because you are providing them with "cheap money," which they loan out at much higher rates. Other highly profitable banking services include renting a safe-deposit box and using the bank as the executor of your estate. Think of it: a small deposit box takes up less than one cubic foot of bank space. Let's say you're paying $15 a year rental for such a box. That's like paying a monthly rent of $80,000 for the average-size one-bedroom apartment in New York City. The point is, by being such a provider for a bank you're an extraordinary tenant. In fact, to obtain a loan today, you must be prepared to open at least a checking account and perhaps even rent a safe-deposit box with the bank you want to grant the loan. While it may not make sense for you to make use of all of a bank's services, you should keep in mind that you are considered a good customer to the extent that you contribute to its profitability.

THE IMPORTANCE OF A CONTACT— YOUR SHEPHERD

A good personal connection is your best means of introduction to the right bank for you. Like most businesspeople, bankers become enormously more comfortable when there is an intermediary, a third party between you and themselves. This can be a family member, friend, boss, or co-worker who has a successful relationship with a specific person in a bank and is willing to introduce you to that person. Preferably, this contact has a presentable balance in his or her checking or savings account.

The right introduction can be magic; it provides the banker with a context, a sense of common ground, and establishes a certain "comfort level" of trust for your budding relationship. For example, a young man confided that he was continually turned down for bank credit. We told him to "get a shepherd" at the bank. The "shepherd" he eventually found wrote on his application, "This is a very good customer of the bank. Any questions, please contact me." The bank started him off with both a line of credit on his checking account and a VISA card. Having a shepherd also saves the banker from the embarrassment of having to quiz you on why you selected his bank. Your mutual acquaintance establishes your legitimacy and character and hould fortify your psyche in adopting a confident, respe ;ful repose toward your potential lender. If possible, try to persuade your contact to call on his or her banker and say, "I have convinced my friend to come to your bank first."

Your shepherd can prove useful in other credit applications besides bank loans. For instance, a widow, age 50, who had never had any of her own credit, told us she was applying for a Carte Blanche card. We told her that she needed something extra for her application to be approved and suggested she staple letters from her broker and banker to her initial application. She did it and later phoned to say she received the card.

How do you find and select your introduction? There are many possible sources. Easily the best contact is one made through a close personal friend or business acquaintance who has a healthy bank account at the particular branch where you will be applying, and who has enjoyed a long and fruitful business and personal relationship with the manager. Gathering such information from a friend or close business associate is usually not as hard as it initially seems. Many people on solid financial footing are sought out by bankers to help insure continued business and in the hopes that they will refer friends to their bank. By giving you his or her banker's name and number, your contact's ego is being gratified while actually helping this person to provide the banker with a lead for new business—you.

Try to find out as much as possible about the banker from this friend—likes, dislikes, whether it's golf, bowling, gardening, or bridge, and other habits as well as his or her overall modus operandi in business. If you are lucky enough to have access to such a golden entrée, show your great appreciation for this interest in your affairs. As long as you do not become burdensome, he or she may become emotionally drawn into your loan request and help push it through with another phone call later on.

While everyone obviously is not graced with such well-heeled friends, most people do know someone—no matter how casually—who can serve admirably as a necessary introduction. Try someone with whom you do business on a regular basis—it could be your employer, your local store-keeper, or your doctor or dentist. Phrase your request along these lines: "I've been thinking of changing banks. I've always admired your business ability. Could you recommend a bank for me?" Once this person has given you the name of his or her own bank—most people will gladly oblige you—try to get him or her to arrange for an appointment with this friend at the bank on your behalf. Remember that everyone in business has a banker. Approach a friendly business proprietor with whom you have maintained a steady relationship, and it will almost certainly lead to a solid introduction to a banker.

Even if this "impersonal contact" merely gives you the name of the bank and branch location, this alone entitles you to call the manager and say, "So-and-so recommended that I come to see you." Defusing the banker's circumspection by establishing a comfortable connection can work with little more than name-dropping. Some time ago, I instructed one of my students to try walking into a branch office of Consolidated Edison (New York City's electric utility) to find out which bank it used, along with the names of both Con Edison's bank representative and the bank officer's name. Armed with this information, he obtained immediate entrance into the bank manager's private office by stating, "Mr. So-and-so from Con Edison suggested I contact you." Of course, it can just as easily open doors if you mention the name of your local hardware store owner or priest. Just find the most prestigious person you know—and, if necessary, force an introduction.

Do not be deterred if your introduction and the banker are above you—the rule is, the better the banker, the better hands you are in. You should only find yourself without an introduction when there is but one bank in town—and you're the town drunk. Then you've got a problem. Even so, if you appeal to the banker's sense of morality—"I'm at your mercy"—the bank would almost certainly be happy to offer you recommendations to other banks close by.

In fact, using one bank to get an introduction to another can be a good gambit. I personally tested this approach and it worked like a charm. I went to a savings bank, supposedly seeking "general information." Once engaged with a banker, I asked, "Can you recommend a commercial bank for a checking account and other accommodations?" (Note the choice of the ambiguous word "accommodations.") He replied, "Of course, National Bank gives consumer accommodations." With this bona fide if tenuous recommendation from a specific banker, I walked into the commercial bank and said, "You were recommended to me by Joe Brown at Savings Bank on Main Street." Since they belonged to the same banking fraternity, it got me beyond the stranger-off-the-street status.

Another variation of this bank-to-bank means of introduction can be obtained by visiting a nearby branch of your neighborhood bank. Once there, have a chat with one of the loan officers sitting behind a desk to discuss his or her thoughts on borrowing. Ask for some general advice: What is considered a reasonable amount to ask for considering your income and expenses? What types of loans does he or she give special attention to? What are the usual terms? As you are about to leave, ask for a business card "for future reference." Once again, you can parlay this introduction by going back to your neighborhood branch and using his or her name as your introduction. Even if you have a suitable introduction through some other means, talking to a banker who is intimately familiar with your bank's current operations, yet removed from the actual review of your loan application, can provide you with important additional insights for casting your application in the best possible light.

A word of caution regarding talking to the banker about your introduction—unless you have unbounded admiration and affection for your mutual connection, keep it short and sweet. If you do not know your introduction well, simply state that you are on good terms with the individual and respect his or her business judgment. Mention that it was your mutual contact who advised you to seek out the banker and that you are hopeful of establishing a good relationship. Listen carefully to what the banker has to say about your introduction. If it is less than glowing, if there are mixed emotions about his or her character or achievements, this is a clear signal for you to forget about dealing with this banker. Just stand up, saying, "Well, _____ spoke highly of *you*," and leave. If the banker's comments were really not that offensive, and if he or she is blushingly repentant, it may work in your favor to let the banker convince you to sit down again. Then again, maybe your introduction is not as strong as you thought, and you would be better off walking out and working on a better contact elsewhere.

Once you are satisfied that you have a respectable introduction to a bank, you should make the effort to find out more about the bank before you proceed with the appointment with the banker. Make sure, for instance, that the bank has a current policy of making consumer loans. Bank policies shift and change dramatically at times; some commercial banks have completely closed down their consumer lending division or have moved most of their customer loan officers into commercial or business banking. Other banks will not consider a loan request for under $2,500. They have decided that it's just not worth their time. In some markets, savings and loan associations are still not willing to exercise their power to grant consumer loans. To avoid a potential waste of your time, you can usually get an answer over the phone regarding policy on unsecured loans and minimum amounts.

Recognize that the banking industry is undergoing a tremendous change, especially among the "money center" banks, the huge commercial banks that have global networks or aspirations. Disregard the fancy media campaigns and look at how long the lines are at your local branch. In many urban areas, major branches of these big commercial banks clearly favor their commercial customers.

Drop into a number of banks for a few minutes to compare and note ambience. Is it a stuffy environment? Are the tellers cheerful? Are the employees relaxed or stiff? Do they wear sports clothes, or is the dress code along the more traditional banking style? In all of these respects and others, formulate impressions of the branch manager in particular. The manager, after all, is your standard; your aim is to identify with his or her style and demeanor.

In the course of stalking your bank, pick up the literature that is on display. Also, ask a teller for the latest annual report. It is helpful to read through both types of bank publications—the display pamphlets tell you what type of loans and other services they are soliciting while the annual report usually notes with pride what accounted for its profit margin and dividend. You can use this information along with any other news about the bank that you have learned in your conversation with your prospective banker. But more about that later on.

NOTEWORTHY BANKS
In today's borrowing environment, certain types of banks have demonstrated a greater receptivity to granting unsecured consumer loans.

Banks with Which You Already Have a Relationship.
These banks are the simplest to approach, provided that
you have maintained an orderly account. The longer you
have held a satisfactory savings or checking account here,
the stronger position this puts you in. By virtue of your
years of loyalty, you have a right to expect personal attention and courteous treatment. Your obvious strength here is
your accomplished demonstration of stability, the single
most important criterion to many creditors. You should
dwell on this setting down of roots in the community when
you meet with the manager, and be sure to mention in pass-
ing any friends and acquaintances that you know are customers of the bank, especially wealthy ones. However, if
you have bounced more than one check here within the last
three years, your creditworthiness is most probably tar-
nished in their eyes. One bad check you should be able to
explain away (the loan officer just might ask you to account
for it during the loan interview, so be prepared), but two or
more notices of insufficient funds starts to look very shaky;
bankers are prone to view these indiscretions as violations
of your hallowed relationship of trust and as a bad basis for
the consideration of any credit. So if you have not been
particularly adept at balancing your checkbook and have
passed bad checks in the recent past, you probably would
do better going elsewhere and starting off with a clean
slate.

Foreign-Owned and New.   Many of these newly formed or
arrival banks seem to care more about the American consumer. Unlike many stodgy domestic banks that are smug
and paternalistic about their retail banking division, foreign
banks are still formulating their policies and are not bur-
dened with deep-seated prejudices. Moreover, they have an
active stake in and a commitment to establishing a foothold
in this country and building their share of the market. If
well managed, these banks tend to hire more entrepre-
neurially oriented employees who look for new opportunities and try harder to accommodate new customers. Today,

these banks are often the leaders in developing new incentives and other devices to attract both deposits and loans, along with other banking services. It's worth a visit to see what they can offer you.

Job-Oriented or "Membership."   Created to support middle America, these institutions focus on serving a specific occupational line or special situation. They include New York's Amalgamated Bank (unions), women's banks, farm banks, credit unions, co-ops, and so on. If you are a member or are eligible to become a member of a credit union or any union of considerable size, this is probably your best credit connection. Most members are entitled to and receive a much warmer reception to a request for an extension of credit—and frequently at much better rates—than a commercial bank will be able to offer you. They most likely have met and worked with other borrowers with circumstances very similar to your own and, therefore, understand and sympathize with your situation, point of view, and proof of ability and willingness to repay.

Certain banks and bank branches develop similar sensitivities by virtue of being situated in communities or neighborhoods with a significant percentage of one type of professional or jobholder—artists, actors, designers, people in media, engineers, or waiters and bartenders. These banks, often out of need, develop specialists in making loans to specific types of people. Whether you live in these communities or not, you should consider locating and identifying banks that fit these occupational niches. Try approaching one saying, "I've heard that you are particularly interested in developing relationships with _____ ." In other words, if you want to open up a Chinese restaurant in a fashionable suburb, you might do well to visit a bank in the Chinatown area as well as ones in your own town.

Banks That "Need" You.   Most consumer-oriented banks go through business cycles or develop new strategies where they are reaching out aggressively for more customers, or for certain types of customers. Be attentive to newspaper ads announcing new banking campaigns and try to hit these "target lending" cycles, be they geared toward mortgages, travel loans, car loans, whatever. Tear out the newspaper ads placed by the "needy" banks and present them to the banker when you meet, saying, "Here I am." Remember, you are not just borrowing the bank's money; you are helping the bank satisfy its need to create successful consumer loans (with the accompanying interest) and discharge its corporate responsibility. It needs you.

Another candidate needy bank might be one located in a depressed area. If you live in a different, more affluent locale, you probably will be considered a better risk than the people in the bank's own immediate market. What makes for a pauper on Park Avenue may seem like a king in Brooklyn.

One-Man Banks.   It's a pleasure to deal with a smaller bank where the president is readily available. I recently dealt with a bank in Putnam county where the president opened the mail and answered the telephone himself. I called up asking to talk with the president and he answered, "Speaking." I was able to get answers on a mortgage application immediately, and was happy to discover how well banking can work unencumbered by layers of "management."

Often, such a small bank is the only bank in town that will grant new church or temple mortgages. This is another good demonstration of smart caring. The bank that maintains its roots, that recognizes its quasi-public obligations, is a bank worth approaching. Check with new religious organizations to see what bank financed construction of their buildings.

Finally, if you are a relative newcomer in a community, you might wish to establish your banking credentials based on a reference from your former bank—provided you have enjoyed a good working relationship with said bank. But don't count on this recommendation coming easily. Banks are not in the habit of providing such recommendations to other banks even when the customers are millionaires. They are typically timid; banks seem to perceive that a written recommendation may be troublesome for legal or ethical reasons. So if you do ask for a reference from your previous bank, make sure you see it in writing before submitting it with your application, because unless you fight for a good one, the recommendation probably won't be especially outstanding.

MAKING THE APPOINTMENT

Now that you have established the best means of introduction for your best prospect bank, call up the banker directly (get his direct line from the bank's main office, if need be) and arrange for an interview. Explain that your mutual associate highly recommended him to advise you and discuss with you financial planning (never "problems") and other services in the hopes of establishing a good relationship with his or her bank. It is important to convey to the banker in this first phone conversation that you consider him or her to be an expert in his field yet you are approaching him as a peer. You should cater to his ego by suggesting that he—by virtue of the high marks granted by your mutual friend—has your confidence in his ability to deal forthrightly with you. This helps earn his trust and makes him feel that he is a person of worth—worthy to work with a person of your worth.

A secretary or other subordinate may intercept your call saying that Mr. or Ms. Big is all tied up. When this person tries to steer you to another banker or asks what is the nature of your call, do not become anxious or haughty in your insistence on speaking with your contact. Politely thank him or her for the interest, introduce yourself as an acquaintance of one of their customers who suggested that you make an appointment with Mr. Big, and ask if next Thursday afternoon would be convenient. If the person says that he or she does not know your banker's schedule, reply that you'll call back later, but leave your name and number. Make sure you get the name of the person you have been speaking with and thank him or her by name. (You never know—this clerical person might wind up scoring your application.)

When you make the appointment to talk with your prospective banker, try to avoid the times of the day, week, and month that are most hurried and thus nonconducive to a relaxed, uninterrupted meeting. Early mornings and late afternoons are filled with many time-consuming banking chores and should be avoided if possible, along with the rush during noon hours. Monday is the worst day generally (back-to-work-and-not-so-happy-to-be-here); people act tougher and are more compulsive about their jobs. They feel they haven't accomplished anything yet. And Friday (the-body-is-present-but-the-mind-has-left-for-the-weekend) may not be the most propitious time to try to engross the weary banker with your concerns. Be aware also that the first three business days of each month are usually hectic times because many customers come in to cash or deposit monthly payroll checks and social security and welfare checks. Additionally, the fifteenth of the month, or the first business day thereafter, is a frenetic time at many banks because a lot of people get paid then. Finally, try to avoid making an appointment for the day before a bank holiday.

The ideal times to schedule an interview are on Wednesday or Thursday, after lunch, between the fourth working day and the middle of the month to the end of the month. Because most bankers are notoriously lunch oriented, early or midafternoon is probably the best time to strike. The banker has had the midday meal—including possibly a couple of drinks—he is sated and relaxed, and consequently he is as amenable (and susceptible) to your powers of persuasion as he is ever going to be.

PREPARING FOR THE MEETING

On the day you see your banker, prepare yourself as if you were going on a job interview. Be well rested; make sure you have a good breakfast and a light lunch. Avoid all mood changers—be it a drink, a joint, or a pill. You don't need any "chemical help" to brace yourself for this meeting. Besides, it will certainly work against you because even if the banker does not suspect it, your mental faculties will become dissipated in wondering whether the person across the desk can tell you are acting artificially. The point is that if you do not feel well physically or emotionally, postpone the appointment—the lender should never see you as a sick, injured, or "defeated" person.

Dress properly. If you are a mechanic or a farmer, you do not necessarily have to wear a tie and jacket if they make you feel uncomfortable, but do not show up in soiled overalls. Don't go to the other extreme either and overdress— flashy jewelry or too much cologne can be just as obnoxious. Make sure you are well groomed and do not wear tinted glasses. (I once knew a banker who said repeatedly that he never trusted anyone with tinted glasses—"he's hiding something, and it's probably drinking.") Don't chew gum or suck on lozenges, and smoke only if the banker smokes first—and then do not ask for permission. In general, do not carry or wear anything that would distract the banker from looking just at you. (I remember thinking that a person carrying a newspaper with him looked like he was searching for a job. Of course, it's a wild assumption, but bankers are trained to make mental notes on meeting people that often develop into pet peeves or downright paranoia.) Don't introduce any unnecessary surprises, like bringing along an infant or a miniature poodle: bankers hate being surprised by people they don't know. Lastly, do not bring this book to the appointment or admit to reading it. That might undermine all your efforts toward presenting yourself properly.

Once you are prepared, you should be in the proper

frame of mind to meet the banker—preparing, in itself, will help create the right attitude. Familiarize yourself with some of the jargon of banking as it pertains to your credit request. Try to learn the meaning of words like amortization, APR, prime rate, simple and discounted interest rates (see Glossary). Do not become overwhelmed, however, by the verbiage of finance or feel compelled to spout this new-found jargon in conversation. It is more important simply to read the newspaper daily, be up on the general business climate, and know what is the bank's current prime rate. You want to be able to convey to your banker that you are an aware, thinking person.

Beyond this bit of preparation, you should recognize that you are probably better prepared for this meeting than for any other business meeting you have ever had—because the subject of this meeting is *you,* and on that subject you are the world's greatest expert. There's absolutely no reason to be nervous; rather, concern yourself with the other person's comfort.

THE MEETING

When you meet the banker, be prepared to meet your equal. While bankers may or may not be cut from the same mold as you are, they do face similar personal and professional struggles. Banking today is a high-visibility industry handling a highly emotional commodity—money. Constant exposure to the public and the added pressure of having to act as if they were immune from making mistakes often cause bankers to appear superior and stiff. And yet, this perception of invulnerability is accomplished by more second-guessing than in almost any other profession: bankers are scrutinized by their peers, their myriad bosses, federal and state examiners, the business press, various industry associations largely dependent on bank financing, and antagonistic consumer protection groups. Being a banker is a tougher job than ever before in this volatile and expanding environment of financial services. The banker is in the very midst of the so-called corporate rat race.

Start the meeting by stepping forward, extending your hand, and introducing yourself confidently. It's okay to smile if you feel like it. Remember that you are coming to the banker in the interests of communication, not supplication. Repeat your telephone conversation introduction about your mutual friend and acknowledge that it is on the basis of his or her appraisal that you thought it would be a good idea to meet. Briefly describe yourself, beginning with the most stable aspect about your life, whether it's your job, address, or occupational field. In other words, if you have just changed jobs and have moved from California to New York but are still an electrical engineer, say that you have been an electrical engineer for the past 10 years, have been married for five years, and have recently upgraded your professional standing and salary by taking on your present job. Tell the banker what your gross income is (including all the other sources summarized in the following chapter). With this introduction, you can now state unabashedly that you are considering taking out a loan.

Make sure you mention that your purpose in meeting today is not to have the loan application decided upon then and there. Rather, it is to talk about your loan application in the context of your overall financial planning. You want to demonstrate that you have prepared the loan application with a great deal of care. Tell him or her that you are here to sign your completed application for the loan after talking it over. Moreover, you wish to assure yourself that your loan application will not be treated mechanically; you want to be certain that the loan application is as clear as possible, and that the banker will accept your loan application and shepherd it through the loan process.

Treat the banker like the professional he or she is. If the banker is of the opposite sex, the same rules apply—keep flirtation out of this. You are there because you need the advice of an expert. Explain that you are concerned about

how you filled out the loan application. You want to be absolutely sure that it's as clear and complete as possible *before* you submit it—and you would appreciate it if the banker would review it with you and give you an opinion as to
the completeness of the application.

GOOD AND BAD LOAN PURPOSES

Don't interrupt when the banker is reviewing the application. Look at the banker, listen hard to his or her comments. The banker will probably want to talk with you
about the purpose of the loan. It's a favorite way of breaking the ice.

In general, a bank looks favorably upon loans that upgrade your lifestyle (within reason) and contribute to your
stability, like furniture, home improvements, and so on.

Here is a list of bad reasons for taking out a loan. Each
one is certain to be viewed by the banker with circumspection and, unless you have put up some solid collateral or
have already demonstrated a high degree of creditworthiness, will most likely result in denial of the loan.

1. loan to relend to someone else
2. an extravagant gift
3. loan that will create another obligation (e.g., a $1,000
loan for a down payment on a $5,000 watch)
4. loan dealing with a business that has nothing to do
with, or is alien to your present income, especially one that
proposes to replace your income stream
5. loan to pay a fine or penalty
6. loan for any reason predicated on an unreasonable
future expectancy ("My rich uncle Henry is expected to die
six months from now; could I borrow $10,000 please?")
7. loan for your own psychiatric care or any reason
connected with your unstable mental health
8. loan to help finance political or unconventional
cause

9. debt consolidation loan (unless the current interest rate is *less* than rates of outstanding loans)

This list is by no means exhaustive, but it does illustrate some of the unacceptable reasons for a loan that bankers have gotten requests for. Strong reasons for granting a loan with little or no reservations (provided, of course, that all other criteria are satisfied) include:

1. loan to improve or establish your credit
2. loan to improve an existing asset (e.g., loan to replace a boiler)
3. medical treatment for some close relative
4. dental and conventional medical treatment for yourself or your family
5. fees for child adoption
6. education loan, especially continuing education

You should realize that your reason for a loan can subsequently change. Once you have been approved for a loan—unless it is collateralized, like a car or boat loan—you can decide to use the money for whatever reason you choose. And some banks are not at all interested in learning what the loan is for, simply judging your credit request on the basis of their formulas as they apply to your situation.

Be sure to bring up any inconsistencies between your credit report and your application if you still have any disputes. Remember that many bankers cannot handle surprises. You do not want them to come across any unexplained item or inconsistency in your credit profile later on, since many banks use these credit reports as the principal means of checking the veracity of your loan application.

YOUR LATENT POWER OF INDIFFERENCE
A particularly effective tool to help establish your character in the eyes of the banker is your power of indiffer-

ence. People who do not appear to be especially concerned about their fate—who are calm, confident, and cheerful in spite of ordinarily trying circumstances—tend to inspire confidence in others. All the world wants to be associated with a winner, and the financing community is certainly no exception. A banker is trained to want to jump on the bandwagon if he or she thinks that another bank is perfectly willing and eager to grant you the loan, and that what you are more concerned about is getting the best rate. You can signal this ambivalence and use your power of indifference by stressing your interest in establishing a superior banking relationship rather than settling on the run-of-the-mill service available elsewhere. Caution: Ambivalence does not mean arrogance. The power of indifference does not imply that you are not a caring person—you have already demonstrated this by your preparation and presence—but that you feel a confidence in knowing that a show of reciprocity is certain from someone, if not the loan officer across the desk. Bankers perceive this as your power to turn to the competition.

A famous Florida real estate tycoon who subsequently filed for bankruptcy with $200 million in debts used to host "hungry bankers" who flew into town from all over the United States. He was courted by these bankers (only later was it recognized that he was seducing them) in large part because of his ability to exude confidence and indifference. As he presided over grand (wet-bar-equipped) helicopter tours pointing ambiguously at various real estate parcels, he would state that he and his projects were moving fast and that, if they wanted a piece of the action, he might be able to convince his other banks to let them share the additional financing. Bank after bank gladly hopped on board; it was fashionable. When his financial mountain of mirrors finally caved in, approximately 150 banks and the IRS were left holding worthless pieces of paper and little else. My point is obviously not to endorse this sort of deception; it could prove to be criminal. The lesson here is that bankers are often encouraged by and respond to your power of in-difference.

Try to present yourself in ways that the banker will be able to identify with—that is, indicate stability—but do not heap on extraneous puffery. Maintain a certain humility and directness of purpose: you want your application reviewed in due deference to the bank's just expectations. If the banker says, "Our rules are _____," your answer should be, "That is why I'm here, to explain how I fit into (or between) those rules." Never let "The Rules" dissuade you. Rules can't work all the time (remember the adage: the exception proves the rule); so, no matter what the official bank policy is, there is always the Rule of Reason—you are entitled to a loan if you can demonstrate that you can pay it back under the bank's terms.

If differences in opinion should arise in conversation, make sure that you never characterize your banker as being unfair or unkind in his judgment. Do not come across as self-righteous and say that he is wrong. Phrase your disagreements in terms of seeing matters in a different light. Your prospective banker is not your opponent—do not turn your meeting into a combat session or a contest of oneupsmanship. You are there to explain yourself and to reach out.

Use your meeting to create a relationship of trust between yourself and the banker. How is this done? Show that you care about him or her, as a person and as a banker. Ask how long he has worked there, why did he choose to become a banker, what satisfaction does he get out of it? Be eager to hear his success stories. Be solicitous. How would he characterize his branch? How do business and community conditions affect the bank? What other banking services does he feel are particularly good for the customer? These questions obligate him to give an extended commercial for the bank, perhaps even a tour. Act fascinated through it all. The vault used to be the pride and joy bankers pointed to at the culmination of their tours. Now it is likely to be their computer operations. Your attitude will go a long way toward determining how long your meeting will last.

How long should you stay? I found myself believing, when I was a loan officer, that a loan meeting was an investment in time and that the longer the meeting took (if it was amicable), the more I was to feel that I should make my investment pay off by granting the loan. Try to get your loan officer to make that investment in time on your behalf.

As you conclude the meeting, ask yourself if you think it went well. If you feel strongly that it did *not* develop positively, retrieve your unsigned application, and take it out of the banker's hands or off the desk. Politely explain that you would rather not submit your application only to get an inquiry notation on your credit profile not followed by the granting of credit. When the banker counters that it might still be possible that your loan will be approved, answer simply that you would rather not gamble.

In more positive circumstances, ask the banker how he felt the meeting went. Respond in kind and thank him for his time, thoughtful guidance, and professional expertise. Reiterate that you appreciate his willingness to act as the shepherd of the loan application.

The last thing you do is sign the application. Perhaps he would be good enough to put his initials on the application with a note to see him if there are any questions. Leave your business card, if you have one, and tell him to feel free to call you in the event that something else comes up that he needs to know—you are sure you can supply anything else he needs.

Finally, tell him that you are very pleased that your mutual acquaintance suggested him as your banker. You want him to know that he has done an excellent job in making things very comfortable for you, and that you feel confident about the prospect of creating a good and growing relationship with your bank and banker.

Chapter Five

Shaping
Your Loan
Application

FILLING OUT YOUR LOAN APPLICATION IS LIKE CREATING A WINDOW on your life. The document you produce speaks for you in your absence; by describing your life with precision and care, you can admirably demonstrate your capacity and personal character. The window of your life must be big, bright, and clear enough for you to look good. There are many pitfalls to avoid and, in extreme cases, you may even have to change certain things about yourself or your lifestyle in order to prove that you can reasonably meet your monthly loan payments. This chapter guides you through the minefield of questions on your loan application, showing you how to defuse or circumvent the likelihood of clerical obliteration by scoring poorly.

The underlying premise of any application for credit is to provide a forum for the "objective" evaluation of risk. In these days of heightened lender skepticism due to historically high delinquency and default rates, as well as bloated levels of interest charges, your application is scrutinized more critically than ever before. Not only does your lender look for a sufficient and stable stream of income, but increasingly more important is any and all evidence regarding your willingness to repay and dependability in this respect. Symptomatic of being creditworthy is scoring well and the absence of negative credit experience. Yet while you may not be able to satisfy this textbook definition of creditworthiness, you can substitute and/or attack the traditional suppositions for which bankers are trained. You can break all the rules and fail all the formulas and still ultimately prevail in proving yourself creditworthy as long as you can show how you can repay your debts.

Most bank loan applications look the same. Sometimes the only difference is the color. They all want you to tell them your net salary, living accommodations, debts, bank accounts, and other personal information. These personal characteristics of yours are then judged primarily according to an optimal level of stability, or the length of time that you have satisfactorily maintained these relationships.

In order to qualify for your loan today, you are supposed to satisfy certain bank formulas derived from their experience with both successful and unsuccessful loans in the past. Unfortunately, these traits tend to become self-perpetuating and restrictive as time goes by, typically lagging behind significant economic and social changes by as much as five years. Accordingly, officers are nearly all free to review loan applications and they can override or reverse a denial caused by a low score, thereby preserving the latitude astute bankers use when making credit judgments. But as was mentioned earlier, bank policies are increasingly dictated by improving economies of scale, which translate into reducing their risk. For a growing percentage of Americans who cannot, or have chosen not to, possess the traditional characteristics of stability due to greater economic volatility or new opportunities, literal answers to certain questions on the loan application will result in a poor score.

Obviously, a scoring system that regards stability as its top priority cannot be the name of the game for all people. But what do you do if you are not a sedentary company custodian putting in your 30 or 40 years until retirement? Why should you be penalized for your versatility, depth of experience, and willingness to face new challenges? Many banks will inadvertently short-change your creditworthiness if left to their own scoring devices. Your solution involves a preemptive first strike that redefines your stability as a function of your frame of mind rather than as an arbitrary length of time.

SUPPLEMENT YOUR ANSWERS

The loan application form provides precious little space to answer the 20 to 35 questions typically asked. Banks want short answers to specific questions to keep their paperwork to a minimum and to "maximize" their ease in scoring. The way to short-circuit the clerical scoring of your application is to obscure and/or embellish your answers to certain problematical questions by providing supplementary explanations. Simply write in the spaces supplied to answer questions like, "How long have you lived at the present address?", "See Supplement A," or your answer with an asterisk referring the clerk to Supplement A. As long as your application is completed neatly—a tidy appearance is very important psychologically—and you have answered all their pertinent questions in your supplements, if not on the application form itself, you can stymie the scoring process without hurting your loan review. In fact, by including additional data in a concise and professional way, your banker (provided he sees the application) is likely to be impressed tremendously by your initiative. Moreover, such care shows appreciation for his or her critical function as a loan officer.

A former student wrote to tell us just how effective supplements to an application can be:

> My husband and I were recently involved in purchasing a brownstone in Brooklyn. Even though we were

sure we had good credit, we were recently married, had lived in New York for less than three years, and my husband had just started his first job as an attending surgeon after ten years of training. So we weren't exactly "stable" according to the banking industry (even though we earn a large income and have paid our bills on time) since we lived in two countries and three states within the recent past.

However, with your help, we overcame. We added appendices to every question on the application that dealt with stability—lengthier answers than the two lines given to explain. We then called our banker, cornered him at his desk at 2:45 P.M. on a Friday afternoon and presented him with our total of *seven* pages of mortgage papers inclusive of appendices, yearly budget, copies of last pay checks, and recent tax returns filed.

In six weeks we received a 90% mortgage from the bank at their preferred customer rate.

Always put your best foot forward. Be careful not to overdo it, however. Rambling supplements that suggest your wholesale disregard of questions asked on the application are likely to bounce back as a denial due to insufficient information.

Let's go down a typical loan application form and review how you should answer the questions:

Name/Address/Social Security No., Etc. Basic information the bank wants in order to identify you. Other personal information banks commonly ask for includes date of birth, driver's license number, and mother's maiden name. Unless you have a very common name or one that can be confused with another member of your family, this personal data is not really essential for the application to be reviewed. (Exception: When applying for an auto loan, a bank may legitimately need your driver's license number.)

Most people do not seem to mind including this superfluous information.

Despite severe restrictions imposed on banks and other institutions regarding the further use of this information, an increasing number of people are reticent to supply what they conceive to be extraneous and unnecessarily personal information. If you are hesitant about filling out some of these spaces, don't. However, you should be aware that some banks will automatically reject such applications as having insufficient documentation *unless* a clearance or other override is initialed in by a loan officer. Be sure to tell your banker during your interview (see prior chapter) that you do not consider such information germane and ask if this will present any problems. It is perfectly appropriate to gently challenge your potential creditor—but don't act paranoid. In fact, if he or she is a stickler about knowing your mother's maiden name, this may be a tipoff that he or she may be an inflexible banker who overrelies on scoring and playing by the book. Seriously consider withdrawing your application.

Residence: Home Ownership Versus Rental.   As a measurement of stability, banks always perceive it to be better to own your house or apartment than to rent. The number of years spent at your present address is also very important, with some banks giving you no additional points in scoring until you have resided for four and a half years in the same place. If you have made a move in the last four years, therefore, you are likely to be penalized to a certain degree. One way to compensate is to say "See Supplement" in the applicable space and type a short paragraph explaining why you have moved. Here are some examples:

> For 12 years, I rented an apartment on Spruce Street in Detroit. After I got married two years ago, my spouse and I bought a house in the suburbs in a good school district with an FHA assumable mortgage at 9%.

Since graduating from college, I have worked for IBM in various capacities for 14 years. IBM transferred me three times during these 14 years with a promotion and sizable salary increase on each occasion. When I was relocated to Houston two months ago as part of our 10-year expansion plan in the south, IBM provided partial financing for my new house.

After living for 27 years in a five-bedroom colonial in Princeton, N.J., we moved last year to Naples, Fla., into a luxury condominium for considerably less than the price of our Princeton home, thus improving our liquidity.

In order to establish an image of psychological stability despite a past of many moves or—in the case of younger consumers—too little past at all, be sure to stress your "roots." If your family is from another part of the country—say, Hicksville—put your present into a context of upward mobility and commitment to your new living arrangement. If your recent move was from a nearby community where you lived for a relatively long time, say that in your supplement. And if you have moved around a lot, account for your living arrangements for the last five years even if the application does not provide for it. You want to show the bank that you have nothing to hide and that there were good reasons (which you briefly explain) to account for each move. Do indicate that you plan to settle wherever you are presently for the foreseeable future, even if your long-range intentions are uncertain.

By dint of past lending experience, stability is what bankers look for. A long time in a hovel is considered more creditworthy than a short stint in a mansion.

Renting is not considered as desirable as owning by banks in determining loans, regardless of the type of accommodations. Typically, you are accorded half as many points on your score. A big monthly rental is nothing to boast about. On the other hand, if your rent is legally controlled as it is in certain parts of the country, or if you have a long-term lease at low rates, definitely mention it in a supplement. If you are on a waiting list to get into a desirable property, also mention it.

While some banks do not score differently between furnished and unfurnished rentals, you can probably assume that bankers look at people without any furniture or who live in a motel, boardinghouse, or trailer as being more transient, less stable. You can try to turn either situation into a psychological plus by stating in your supplement that (1) it is a fully furnished apartment and you do not anticipate needing any additional furniture or appliances, or (2) while your rental is unfurnished, you have already acquired all the furnishings you desire for the foreseeable future. If you are no longer carrying any finance charges for these purchases, add that fact.

If you have just moved into an apartment within the last six months, don't fill out the space in the application. Refer the bank to the appropriate supplement where you can mention that you signed a two-year lease.

Some loan applications ask if you own other real estate beyond your home. Answer yes whether you own a vacation home or vacant parcel or a cemetery plot. Most forms do not require you to detail the nature of your additional holdings.

Whatever real estate you own with a mortgage, state your ownership in a supplement in terms of the amount of your equity stake—that is, the market value of the property less the remaining debt. If the mortgage rate is appreciably below current market rates include that fact in your supplement. Finally, if you know of the recent sale price of a comparable piece of property nearby, state that as well. Remember, you are including this information to flesh out your financial acumen and substance. Incidentally, do not let an upstart banker goad you into signing your home as collateral.

Employment.   While banks naturally are entitled to know how you earn your salary, they are usually more than a little simplistic and biased in judging this information. Their verification process and general level of concern is a great deal less if you are employed by someone else rather than being self-employed. Traditional experience dictates that self-employed people are more susceptible to wide variances in income, no matter what their occupation. If you work for someone else, all you have to do is bring in your last two paychecks or stubs and perhaps a prior year's W-2 form. That is sufficient verification. The very fact that you work for someone else is in itself verification. It's whom you work for that's important, and the longer you have worked there the better. Often, the bigger the company is the better, not withstanding colossal cripples like the automakers and ailing airlines laying off legions.

If you have been employed less than three years at your present job or if there is a question regarding your previous employment, use your supplement to show stability. List time at your previous job(s) or note school attendance or living at home. Your previous employment (when there are many jobs to choose from) should relate to your current occupation or display the depth of your abilities or commitment. It is generally a good idea to mention that you worked your way through school if you have very recently entered the job market. If you can make a case that you are in the midst of becoming this generation's equivalent of Horatio Alger, working up from the mailroom to the president's suite, do so in an understated, strictly facts-and-dates fashion. In general, eliminate the possibility that you will be perceived as job-hopping by delineating in your supplement how each new position is better than the last. This applies to any career change as well—it's a plus as long as you are making more money and improving yourself. Your answer to nonstability is advancement.

Self-employment is considered slippery by banks. They

are much more comfortable getting a third-party authenti-
cation of your gainful employment than relying on your
word or pressing you for a 1040 tax return statement. Consequently, if you are a part owner or own your corporation,
you should indicate this fact, but still put down on your
application that you are employed by a "third party." The
problem with banks that have hard-and-fast rules about requiring to see your tax return is that this document is typically completed so as to minimize your income through
avoidance (not to be confused with evasion). When you are
self-employed, it is very possible that your 1040 does not
truly indicate your income with the exactitude you would
like it to when applying for a loan. For instance, if you own
a food store, it is more than likely paying for your food bill.
Be prepared to supplement your 1040 with a more accurate
profit-and-loss statement prepared by your accountant or
another third party for the last two years. It is important to
document your business financial portrait for both the past
and the future as well as the present by showing stability
and growth. While bankers assume the economic future of
an employed person, they do not as readily make that assumption about those self-employed. You can make the
banker more comfortable by detailing any long-term contracts or business that repeats on a regular basis.

Salary.   List your gross salary. If space is not provided for
it or if the form asks for your net salary additionally, say
"See Supplement." Your tax savings should be part of your
take-home stream. Whatever tax avoidance methods you
employ should be taken into account in the supplement and
made part of the average.

Other Income.   If you have other income, again you
should detail all the sources in the supplement—but do put
the total amount on the application. Make sure you consider all the following sources: (1) interest from savings account, (2) income from securities and other financial instru-

ments, (3) rents received, (4) annual cash gifts, including those from relatives, (5) cash settlements from litigation, and (6) any one-time or recurring payment to you. In other words, if your purebred English sheepdog is pregnant (and you have the appropriate papers), list the likelihood of an average size litter times the current market value of the puppies in your supplement for "Other Income." For the next 12 months, your sources of income can be itemized in detail; subsequent years can be listed as conservative totals. Any significant long-term contracts should be cited as evidence of stability.

Basically, everyone has two kinds of income. First, monies that come in no matter what: salary, annuities, and so on. Second, monies derived from reasonable expectancies: an annual raise and/or bonus, the sale of something, the return of a deposit, the annual birthday gift, any bona fide third-party cash promise, or the repayment of a debt.

Another important source of future income that should be noted is the end of a recurring expense—that is, your daughter's graduation from college this year, terminating a yearly $10,000 tuition, room, and board bill.

The theory you should apply in this loan application is that you are paying back your debts from all your gathered funds rather than from strictly earned income. Do not let the word "income" throw you off; too many people make the mistake of grossly underestimating their true value in terms of gathered funds and total assets. Although most people and most banks are not aware of this untapped reserve of creditworthiness, your bank must acknowledge it when you bring it to its attention.

Debts. Banks are naturally interested in who your other creditors are, including department stores, other credit and charge cards and credit unions. Mostly, they are interested in checking out your performance regarding repayment and chronically or currently large balances. They want to know what your monthly payment is for each creditor, as well as tax and insurance obligations, in order to see if you qualify for their debt-to-income ratio. In other words, they want to know your requested loan's impact on your monthly payment burden. Specify short-term debts, as bankers will often eliminate them from ratio determinations.

Number and Age of Dependents. While you should fill out this portion of the application, be aware that many banks use this information to gauge your monthly overhead for food and other items. You can use your supplement again to show that some or all of your dependents are either wholly or partially self-supporting. A child away at school on scholarship and/or loans should not be included as part of your overhead.

Purpose. Unless your loan is for a car or boat or home improvement, refer the banker to your supplement where you can explain in greater detail the nature of your objective. Make sure it is not one of the sure turndowns listed in Chapter 4. Debt consolidation is no longer a respectable reason for a loan (unless you get a cheaper interest rate than what you are presently carrying).

Amount of Loan. This is probably the last item you should decide, even after figuring out your budget and balance sheet (see below). The more important criterion to keep in mind is what the monthly payment should be, including interest. There are, of course, maximum recommended indebtedness formulas that banks want you to stay below, but the only rule that is real is that your total monthly payments must be easily available from your demonstrated cash flow.

YOUR YEARLY BUDGET
Another significant criterion banks used to review the creditworthiness of your loan request is a budget formulated

on the basis of some of the information you provided and their own assumptions. For instance, one major commercial bank in New York budgets the cost of food for every member of an applicant's household at $92.50 a month in 1982, and assumes that a reasonable clothing allowance is $40 a month per person. But such generalizations are of dubious value. Some people spend more on vacations and less on food budgets, others splurge on stereo equipment instead of new tires.

To avoid being falsely stereotyped, you must demonstrate your own *peculiar* ability to repay the loan in accordance with its terms. What we are really proposing is that you *back into your loan request.* Here's how you do it: First, add up your

• *Annualized Gross Receipts.* As outlined above, it should include an itemization of every single dollar you can logically and reasonably anticipate.

From this, subtract

• *Annualized Expenses.* Again, as thoroughly detailed as possible, taking into consideration an emergency factor and vacation.

Subtract again

• *Annualized Debt Repayment.* List all debts with 12 months' maturity and longer, footnoting those of shorter maturity in a separate section.

Take 85 percent of the resultant number (a banker's comfort factor) and divide it by 12. That final number is your RCN (Repayment Capacity Number).

Now go to the loan charts that some banks and most stationery stores will provide you with and see what you can borrow on a one-, two-, or three-year basis. Remember, the longer the term, the more you can borrow, but the more costly the interest factor becomes. Also, you can always ask for more and agree to accept less.

The procedure just outlined is identical to basic methodologies employed by major corporate borrowers. Any sophisticated banker would appreciate and admire the reasonable assumptions and practicality of your approach.

YOUR CONSUMER'S BALANCE SHEET

To deliver another impression to the supplement, consider preparing a Consumer's Balance Sheet. This can be an ample substitute for the "low-stability" scorer, who scores low in stability because of youth, or the "late bloomer" in consumer finance. Here you add to a typical balance sheet of assets (real estate, securities, cash) any of these unique assets that most bankers would agree to consider in making worth estimates: (1) personal property in the attic or basement that can reasonably be viewed as "collectibles"; (2) reasonable and logical long-term cash expectancies such as the completion of a book, painting, or musical composition; (3) long-term cash anticipations from family and friends. Of course, you will list legal obligations with your liabilities.

BE AWARE OF THESE FORMULAS

By submitting your own supplement complete with your own budget and possibly a balance sheet, you can effectively prevent the bank from drawing a preemptive conclusion about your situation based on its own assumptions. Still, you should know what they usually are if they happen to make you appear *unstable*.

Upon completing their own budget for you with the requested loan figured in, most banks want to see a surplus of at least 10 percent of your net monthly take-home pay. Presumably, you have taken care of this by calculating only 85 percent of your annualized receipts minus expenses and debt repayment.

Other popular bank loan formulas are: your total installment debt should not exceed 20 to 25 percent of your net take-home pay, and your mortgage or other payments for living arrangements should be a maximum of 25 percent of your net or 33 percent of your gross income.

While these are neat little ditties to sing on cue, they do not apply to the real lending world. Can you imagine a banker trying to constrain a corporate customer to borrowing 25 percent of its net earnings? The cost of credit may be a very good reason why you may not want to borrow in excess of or even close to some of these bank-imposed limits, but any banker who preaches that its policy is not to lend above that ratio is treating you like a child.

The real rule is the Rule of Reason: if you can demonstrate that you can reasonably pay it back, a smart banker or other creditor will lend it gladly. Bankers refer to the potential of a loan payback as an *exit*. A clear demonstration of an exit in his evaluation of your application pleases the banker and means a greater probability of loan approval, scoring and ratios notwithstanding.

THE AUTO LOAN: A CREDIT CASE STUDY

Taking the time to enhance your credit application worked for another client of mine. Here's his story:

"I submitted my auto loan through the auto dealer and developed a personal relationship with the sales person at the dealership, as it appeared that she would be in contact with the people at Citibank.

"I followed your suggestions to personalize the application and also demonstrate traits of prudence and responsibility. Besides the tactic of showing how the purchase was possible because of savings that would occur in

terms of taxes and operating costs, I also discussed the fact
that the car was a good investment because of its high resale value.

"Another trick I used was to mention my wife's income
in the supplement. I did not want to offer her to be a comaker of the loan because her credit history is not as good
as mine. However, I wanted the bank to be aware of her
income so I mentioned it in the supplement rather than in
the application itself."

The Cover Letter

Citibank, N.A.

Dear Loan Officer:

*I have been a Citibank customer for close to ten years
with a checking account, savings account, certificates
of deposit, Checking Plus, MasterCard and VISA.*

*I am submitting with this cover letter my "Buyer's
Statement" relative to a purchase I have contracted to
make with Manhattan Honda. I request that you give
it careful consideration.*

*I am aware that the amount of financing which I am
requesting may be beyond that which the bank would
normally give in relation to my income and monthly
obligations.*

*However, I believe that due to the nature of the pur-
chase which I intend to make and my particular financial position (see my "Supplement to Buyer's Statement"), it would be appropriate for you to grant my
application.*

*If there are any questions or need for further informa-
tion, please call me at _____ .*

Thank you for your attention to this matter.

Very sincerely yours,

Supplement to the Buyer's Statement

Reason for Loan: I require an automobile in the course of my work. The purchase of this car will result in savings in operating expenses and tax deductions which are greater than the yearly loan payments.

Present Car

Operating expenses for present car are per year:

Fuel & oil	$2,430.00
Repairs & maintenance	1,295.00
Total	$3,725.00
Tax deduction	$4,473.00

New Car

Yearly operating expenses for new car:

Fuel & oil	$1,125.00
Repairs & maintenance	475.00
Total	$1,600.00
Tax deduction	$6,903.00, or an additional $2,430.00

Savings on New Car

Reduction in operating expenses	$2,125.00
Tax Reduction (at 45% marginal tax bracket)	1,053.00
Total yearly savings	$3,178.00

Thus, through savings alone, I am able to afford the cost of purchasing the vehicle. As an added factor, the purchase represents a stable investment due to the car's good track of holding up its resale value.

Additional Information to Buyer's Statement Categories

1. Home Address: *My permanent address is as noted. I also maintained an address at _____ for the convenience and at the expense of my employers.*

2. Employment: *I am presently employed with _____ and have been so employed since September, 1975.*

I was employed by _____ from June, 1971 to August, 1980.

I resigned from my former position at _____ to take a higher and better paying position with _____ .

3. Income: *I am retained at a base salary of $____ per year. My profit sharing and commissions are anticipated to be a minimum of $____ .*

In relation to expenses, it would be important to consider that my spouse (who has a base salary of $____ per year plus commissions) pays half of our basic budget items, i.e., rent, utilities, food, entertainment, and other basics.

4. Bank Accounts: *I also maintain an account at Chemical Bank, 199 Church St. Acct. # ____ .*

5. *Fixed Monthly Obligations:*   *I also have a Checking Plus Account attached to my Citibank account. Unpaid balance is $895.78; monthly payments are $50.00.*

IF THERE IS ANY FURTHER INFORMATION NEEDED PLEASE CALL ME AT: _____ .

Chapter Six

Credit Rejection: What to Do

YOU'VE BEEN REJECTED. THE BANK HAS TURNED YOU DOWN. OR perhaps your charge or credit card application has been denied. You're dejected, humiliated, shaken. In spite of all your planning and deliberation, you've been run over by the train of authority. There is a feeling of impotent rage. What now?

Unfortunately, the answer for most Americans is the "shoulder shrug"—mute acceptance of the judgment that's been handed down. That's it; you're finished. Well, that's not it; you should never walk away from a rejection. "No" is not a decision, but a *reaction,* and given more information a different decision could result. Rejection is just a temporary setback or obstacle to overcome. It's merely a warning, a signal that you've got to change tactics. You must take control again.

Not accepting a rejection is *not* fighting the system. It's part of the system: the right to appeal has always been a fundamental, inalienable right within the American system. It is simply part of our culture. We've always treated the right to appeal with reverence and kept it untainted. And even when there is no established procedure for an appeal, you can actually establish your own. The credit granting system is sensitive to people who have been rejected, especially those who may have been rejected capriciously (we have federal laws protecting equal rights to credit, and in many banks a loan application must be turned down by two lending officers). The more savvy the appellate authority, the greater the probability that you will get another hearing—but you must be persistent.

Standing up to a credit rejection is not just a formality of exercising your rights; it's a question of protecting your financial future and your good name. Credit rejection is a serious matter, and it can be quite an injury. If one credit grantor has rejected you, other credit grantors may feel safer in rejecting you—"See, we're not the only ones who rejected you, we're just being consistent." A list of credit rejections that appear often as "Inquiry" lines on your credit bureau report can be chronic hazards to your financial health and reputation, so you *must* fight it. Even if you don't need the credit, you should appeal any rejection because it's not just the money that matters, it's your creditworthiness.

You can't afford to shoulder-shrug your way through life. You must persevere in the face of rejections and you must be resourceful in doing so. The granting of credit is of such singular importance that you must be prepared to spend as much time dealing with a rejection as you did preparing the application—it's that critical. Yet, oddly enough, the whole process becomes simplified as a result of the new and sudden clarity inherent in the rejection—we can now direct efforts toward the person who signed the rejection letter, not toward an anonymous institution.

THE APPEAL

Under federal law, a credit grantor must notify you (orally or in writing) of adverse action taken on your application within 30 days. If you receive a rejection notice, your first step in the appeal process is fact-finding: you need as much information as you can to galvanize a strategy. Find out if there is a formal procedure for reconsidering your application. Many banks will refer you to the lending officer of the local branch that processed your loan, then to the bank's consumer credit office. Play by the rules because if you don't, you'll make people angry and possibly damage your case for fair consideration. If, for some reason, however, there seem to be no set procedures, you are free to establish your own.

THE LETTER OF RECONSIDERATION

In the case of any loan request, including VISA and MasterCard, write the senior lending officer of the bank's consumer division (the president, if you're dealing with a rural or suburban bank); for charge card turndowns, write the consumer affairs group (copy to the president); and in the case of department store cards, write the credit manager (copy to the president). Always address your letters using the actual names of officers, not just "To the President." The substance of your letter should contain a history of transactions with the credit institution, including interviews and dates, and your aim—that you desire a reconsideration of your application. For example:

Mr. Jarvis Lorry
Senior Lending Officer
Tellson's Bank

Dear Mr. Lorry:

I recently received notification from the bank declining my request for a $10,000 consumer loan (see attached) and I am writing to urge your reconsideration of my revised application.

I met with your lending officer, Mr. Jerry Smyth, on March 2, _____ and submitted what I believed was a strong application on March 16. Nevertheless, I realize that the facts presented you may not have been sufficient to warrant positive consideration. Hence, I would greatly appreciate an opportunity to meet with you or your deputy to discuss specific problems with my application and means for remedying any inadequacies.

I will call you in one week to arrange for an appointment. Thank you very much for your consideration.

Cordially,
Sydney Carton

If you get no response to your letter or follow-up phone call, write a second letter, saying that you assume that your first letter (copy enclosed) may not have been acted upon because of other pressing business or perhaps because it was misplaced. Reiterate that you will call within seven days to arrange a meeting. Still no answer? Write a third letter saying that you have been trying to arrange a dialogue with the lender's institution regarding the rejection of your application for credit, which you feel may have been predicated on insufficient facts. Be firm and direct: "Having not heard from you, could it be that your institution has no mechanism by which a consumer can exercise his rights of appeal? Or am I required to have the regional Federal Reserve Bank, the State Banking Department, the Comptroller of the Currency, or some other regulatory agency become my advocate? As a matter of fairness, would you please see that someone is in to talk to me when I call on _____ ? (cc: Consumer Affairs Division, Federal Reserve Bank). A third letter should never be necessary—the possibility of "going public" almost always accelerates a response.

THE WHY

Whether or not there is an established appeals mechanism, you should set up a first meeting with a lending offi-

cer as a fact-finding session. As a consumer, you are entitled to *specific* reasons for rejection of a credit request
under the Federal Reserve Board's Regulation B (Equal
Credit Opportunity). A credit grantor may formulate its
own reason or it may use all or some of the 20 principal
reasons suggested by the Federal Reserve:

1. credit application incomplete
2. insufficient credit references
3. unable to verify credit references
4. no credit file
5. insufficient credit file
6. delinquent credit obligations
7. length of employment
8. temporary or irregular employment
9. unable to verify employment
10. insufficient income
11. unable to verify income
12. excessive obligations
13. inadequate collateral
14. too short a period of residence
15. temporary residence
16. unable to verify residence
17. garnishment, attachment, foreclosure, repossession,
or suit
18. bankruptcy
19. we do not grant credit to any applicant on the terms
you request
20. other—specify

Your rejection notice must list the reason(s) for your
turndown, even if it is the result of credit scoring. It is not
sufficient to say that your overall score simply wasn't high
enough; the credit grantor must give specific reasons—usually listing a handful of categories in which you scored low
(employment stability, residence stability, credit experience, banking experience, income). So once you receive

the declination notice, you should call the credit grantor to confirm that these reasons are in fact the precise ones that resulted in your turndown. With this information in hand, your task is well focused. The Federal Reserve has helped you by requiring specific reasons: now that you have fixed targets, you're actually in a better position to obtain your credit.

THE MEETING

When you meet with the lending officer, ask him or her to elaborate on the adverse action taken on your application. Get as much detail as you can. Don't be timorous, be positive. A credit application is merely an assembly of facts; a rejection, in turn, is just a perception that the facts as they stand don't provide enough positive information to allow a lending officer to say yes. Make the lending officer your ally, your "consultant." In your heart of hearts, you know that you have the capacity and willingness to pay back the loan, but your application apparently failed to demonstrate this—so you'd like to correct this misconception and resubmit your application. How would the lending officer handle it if he or she were you? Many bankers are more than willing to tell you how to qualify; they want to help people secure credit—after all, it literally costs as much to say no as it does to say yes.

In fact, a good banker is never upset by the person who appeals a rejection. "You *should* challenge; too many people don't," says a senior lending officer of a major bank. If there are any questions about the validity of a turndown, they will come out, inevitably, in the light of a rational discussion with the credit officer. Your appeal is a chance to uncover things in the borrowing process that you didn't see before; demonstrate again your sparks of intelligence, caring, and willingness to extend yourself in accommodating the lender's needs as well as your own. You are challenging the turndown because you *care* about your creditworthiness. Your lending officer, perhaps more than any other professional, should appreciate and applaud your concern. And if he or she doesn't—if the officer tells you to go away, then do so—then push the "up" button to see his or her boss to begin the vital appeal process.

20 REASONS FOR REJECTION

Credit Application Incomplete

This should never be a reason for your turndown if you have followed our instructions from Chapter 5 ("Shaping Your Loan Application"). However, if you've chosen not to answer a specific question—and there may be good reasons for not answering (the question is damaging, ambiguous, or not applicable)—you have to explain your reasons for not doing so. Many consumer credit offices will not make a decision on your loan application if they feel it is incomplete in any respect. They will wait until the local branch comes back with the requisite pieces of information. If, indeed, some relevant information is missing from your application, send it promptly to your lending officer. A banker told us: "A couple of days ago I asked this person to send me some information missing from his application. I was out of the office until today, and when I came back, I found the information on my desk. I'm impressed by that."

Credit Experience

- insufficient credit references
- unable to verify credit references
- no credit file
- insufficient credit file
- delinquent credit obligations

Before you meet with the credit officer this time, get a new credit bureau report to make sure nothing has gone awry in your credit history—perhaps something unexpected has crept into your profile. If you are cited for delinquent credit obligations and you see no record on the profile, find out where the company got this information. In the event that information was obtained from an outside source other than a credit reporting agency, you have a right under the Fair Credit Reporting Act to make a written request for the disclosure of the nature of this adverse action.

If you have no credit file, something is wrong—you haven't read Chapter 2 of this book. You should know by now that if you have no credit profile, according to American banks and other credit granting institutions, you don't exist. If, on the other hand, you have insufficient credit references or an insufficient credit file, you have to get more information on what their particular guidelines are. It may be that you have other credit inquiries outstanding and the bank wants to know what happened. This is also an opportunity to offer instances and evidence of credit extended to you by people who do not report to credit agencies—the jeweler on Steinway Street, for example (see again Chapter 2).

Before you submit or resubmit your application, you should attempt to check your credit references to make sure they are verifiable. If there is a reference that cannot be verified (the company is out of business, they've lost your records, etc.), then provide secondary evidence of your credit history, such as the original contract, invoice, or canceled checks.

Employment Experience
- length of employment
- temporary or irregular employment
- unable to verify employment

Questions about your employment should have been handled on the application and during the first interview with the loan officer (see Chapters 4 and 5), so you should not be rejected for these reasons. Your movement from job to job or your less than "stable" tenure at a job should have been explained in the supplements to your application. Make sure that your moving up in a field of expertise while bouncing from job to job is perceived as a continuity of employment growth—this career pattern is perfectly acceptable, once demonstrated, to lending officers. Furthermore, you should consider getting letters of reference from prominent citizens (not family members) attesting to your reliable, consistent character—at this point in the appeals process such personal recommendations may count.

An inability to verify an applicant's employment is not uncommon, especially because the personnel offices of major companies are often unwilling (by reason of law) to say anything about their employees. Since bank people by nature are not too tenacious in pursuing this information, you should check again to make sure that your personnel department is alerted to answer questions on the application. Better yet, make it easy on your creditor by asking the personnel people to forward the information in writing. Do not hesitate to call former employers for this documentation.

Income Stability

- insufficient income
- unable to verify income
- excessive obligations
- inadequate collateral

As indicated in Chapter 5, income does not necessarily mean just money from a salaried job. Whenever possible, enlarge your stated salaried income by adding other gross receipts (free-lance work or other sales) or expectancies. For example, often overlooked yet legitimate sources of income include being a beneficiary to an irrevocable trust, expected income from litigation, works in progress, and money due you from loans.

Conversely, you might counter the charge of insufficient

income by asking for a longer period of time over which you pay back, thus placing yourself within an acceptable debt-to-income ratio. For example, if you obtained a $3,000 loan over one year, the monthly payments might bring you about 25 percent of your net income, violating the generally accepted credit rule-of-thumb: total installment debt, excluding mortgage payments, should not exceed 25 percent of your net disposable income. If, however, you spread the same loan over two years your payments might come to only 20 percent of your income every month—over three years, 15 percent.

If the declination notice cites excessive obligations, and you feel this is not the case, find out what are the "acceptable" formulas. These formulas notwithstanding, the monthly budget in your application should have demonstrated that all your obligations have been paid off with enough money left over to satisfy the newly sought obligations as well as an "emergency fund" and occasional nights out.

Faced with "inadequate collateral," you must open the door to supply more collateral (see discussion in Chapter 5). You should have prepared a consumer's balance sheet of assets and liabilities, indicating your defined, measurable worth and possibilities for collateral: cash, negotiable securities, collectibles, personal property such as furnishings, jewelry, automobiles—the more liquid, the better.

Your income, too, is something that should have been verified in your application, since most corporate personnel offices will not give out this information. Verification is generally demonstrated in your W-2 or 1099 forms—or if you are in business for yourself, your company tax return or an accountant's profit-and-loss statement.

Residence Stability
- too short a period of residence
- temporary residence
- unable to verify residence

The issue of residence, if problematic, should have been handled in your application, and certainly explained at your interview. In general, no matter where you're residing, you should indicate that your intent is to live there permanently. If you are in temporary quarters, awaiting the construction of a new home or the vacating of an apartment you've signed a lease for, indicate this again—this will render "temporary" insignificant.

The inability to verify your residence often arises as an inconsistency between the address given by your credit bureau profile and the residence you have given on your application. Again, you always have to check and correct your credit profile, because if there is a contradiction, bankers get confused and the credit profile usually prevails.

Other Problems

• garnishment, attachment, foreclosure, repossession, or suit
• bankruptcy
• we do not grant credit to any applicant on the terms you request
• other—specify

Any one of these reasons—garnishment, attachment, foreclosure, repossession, suit, or bankruptcy—is reason enough to turn you down, and you should have known that from the beginning. Credit grantors are especially wary of bankruptcies—not only because of the sudden and sharp increase in bankruptcies over the last few years, but also because of a Purdue University study, which found that 40 percent of those who declared bankruptcy could actually have paid their way out of it. If your declination notice indicates a garnishment or attachment and there has been none, ask the credit grantor for evidence—it may be that the information actually applies to someone else with a similar name or that it's just an error (see letter of disputation in Chapter 2).

If the credit institution does not grant credit to "any applicant on the terms you request," all you can do is find out from the lending officer under what terms he *would* grant credit. By modifying your request, you may very well be able to fit into one of its criteria.

If rehabilitating your application to the satisfaction of a credit officer seems a difficult prospect, you should consider bringing in a cosigner or co-obligor. This is not necessarily a strategy of last resort. It is simply a means of "blending out" your background with someone who can better demonstrate the criteria for good credit sought by the lender—not that there is something wrong with you, just that a cosigner might provide the necessary addition to your makeup that you haven't developed yet or cannot demonstrate as readily. Having a cosigner enables you to take a black-and-white picture and give it color, so to speak. It makes things easier for the credit officer because now he or she has another target, a larger "exit"—and, often, if the officer would make the loan to your cosigner, he or she will make the loan to you.

There is nothing embarrassing or repugnant about using a cosigner. It's a common practice in the commercial world—they're called sureties or guarantors, and they are used throughout the insurance field. You should treat your cosigner as you would a professional guarantor: consider paying this person a fee of, say, 5 percent of the principal amount sought. And, assuming you are successful in obtaining the desired credit, you might ask your credit grantor to release the cosigner from liability after several months or a year of demonstrating your ability and willingness to meet each payment punctually.

Once you have completed your fact-finding interview, get back to the credit officer with a "recast" application. Never reapply with the same set of facts, only amended ones. This allows the lending officer to save face while changing his or her mind. The officer is not being forced to reverse a "wrong" decision, but is making a new one based upon a consideration of facts that were not available before.

Attach to your new application a cover letter to be delivered personally to the credit officer. The letter should make reference to the old application for credit, which was rejected for _____ reason, a reason not appropriate to your true circumstances. If, for example, the turndown reason was "temporary residence," respond with, "I should not have been turned down for temporary residence because _____ ." There must be a counter to the charge and some elaboration. By doing this, you obviate the possibility that the credit officer will say, "Well, you were turned down for that reason and that's it."

The rejection of your application has put you in a position of surprising clarity. Gone is your sweeping concern for dozens of details. Now you can concentrate on the few remaining roadblocks. In this sense, the act of rejection has an extraordinary capacity to transform your negative situation into a positive opportunity. You can see clearly now: with this apparent setback, you have specific targets to attack and your chances of landing a loan may, in fact, be better than ever.

THE POWER OF PERSISTENCE

When you meet the credit officer again to make your formal appeal, be polite yet persistent. This is not a conflict; the bank has not made a "mistake" based on the old set of facts. You are here to change an institutional mind based on "new information." With recast application in hand, reestablish your three Cs of credit: you have the *capacity* to pay back the loan (or other credit payments); you have the *character*—the willingness and discipline—to pay back on time; and you have sufficient *collateral,* in the event of extenuating circumstances, to give the credit grantor an "exit." In short, no matter what the specific reason given for the turndown, you have demonstrated that you can pay back the loan, and this is the issue, not any one of 20 items.

Overwhelm the lender with caring. Of course you are concerned about the person's need to protect the bank against delinquencies and defaults (especially today, when the liberalization of the bankruptcy law has been accompanied by a 130 percent rise in personal bankruptcies over the past two years). At the same time, you are concerned about your creditworthiness. The rejection has dealt a blow to your reputation and it's important for you to overturn this "verdict." Don't underestimate the power of persistence. Ultimately, no institution in America can withstand persistence; they're not designed to do so. Be persistent, but not in a gnawing, repetitive way, calculated to drive someone crazy until they say yes. Your lender must understand that you are being persistent because good credit is the clarion of your good name.

Personalize your persistence—make the credit grantor see you, and your chances for success will improve dramatically. Examples of successful persistence abound: A woman applying for a $7,500 car loan (10 percent down) was rejected by the New York bank recommended by the dealer who was selling her the car. The bank said that she was turned down because (1) her credit bureau report listed negative items (late payments) with two department stores, and (2) she had an insufficient credit history (she was recently separated). She called up the department stores and got one of them to remove the negative credit bureau listing—while occasionally late in paying, she was still a substantial and reliable customer. Next, she applied for the loan at her own bank, but again, she was rejected for the same reasons. This time she called up the bank's consumer credit division. She explained her dealings with the department stores and emphasized that she had considerable holdings in real estate (she owned two apartment buildings and had contracts to buy two more). With that sort of collateral, she couldn't understand why the bank had turned her down. The loan officer listened and agreed—she couldn't understand the turndown either—and said she would look into it. A few days later the loan came through, with no downpayment necessary.

Even when credit or charge card companies turn you down, persistence pays off. Many of these companies rely on scoring and may perfunctorily reject you because of low scores in certain categories. But the computers are not brains; they cannot score a personal letter of appeal. Once your letter puts your application back into human hands, you have another chance for fair and rational consideration. Take, for example, the case of a consulting engineer in the northeast who wrote us telling of a Diners Club turndown. "The reason they gave was negative information in my credit file (late VISA payments). I sent them a letter asking to be reconsidered and included an explanation of my history with VISA, Xerox copies of my VISA statements showing regular payments, and a brief sketch of my income and expenses demonstrating my ability to pay. *They sent me a card.*"

CREDIT REVOCATION REINSTATED

Even when your credit is revoked, you can get it back by applying the same rules outlined above. Here's a letter written by a friend of ours that resulted in the reinstatement of her credit card.

Bankcard Products Group
San Francisco, Ca.

Dear Ms. _____ :

I believe my MasterCard account # _____ was cancelled because of a misunderstanding, and errors on my part, and on the part of Crocker National Bank. I would like you to record the following explanation on my permanent record, and consider this information as part of this formal request for reinstatement or reissue of my credit privileges.

Although Crocker Bank claims to have notified me of impending cancellation on December 13th, 1980, I have never received such a notice. I did, however, bring the account up-to-date on December 26th. Seven days later, however, my account was cancelled. I made regular payments on January 18th ($181.28), February 28th ($130), and March 29th ($40). As has been my practice during the 10 years which I have enjoyed the use of a MasterCard, I have made payments in excess of the minimum due.

I understand on several occasions my account exceeded my credit limit, but the excessive amount was small, and in all cases, I brought the account back into order quickly. I'm sure you can understand that it is not always easy to keep a close running total of an account balance when making purchases frequently.

I sent payments of $100, posted by you on July 8th, yet on July 9th you sent me a letter advising that "it is not possible for us to continue to maintain an account in this position. . . . A payment is due within 5 days."

I believe several things have contributed to this unfortunate situation. First, although I have attempted to make regular payments, you have not always credited them before you have sent letters or taken action. There is undoubtedly a delay in the process. Second, I did move, and notified you of my new address. It appears, though, that you received or instituted my address change long after it was sent. I have been living at my current address since December of 1980, have received mail here, and have not had any trouble with other creditors.

My account was delinquent in April and May because I was transferring jobs, and was for a time unemployed. I neglected to inform you of this condition, since at the time it did not occur to me that you would be sympathetic with my predicament, but I realize now that was a mistake.

I realize that credit standards have been tightened, and that your rules are enforced strictly. But I can assure you that it was never my intention to default on my credit obligation. Indeed, I believe that if you review my payment history carefully, you will see that I have in almost all instances proved to be a conscientious customer.

I will admit to making some mistakes in the handling of my account, but I believe you have made mistakes too, which, when compounded, have resulted in an unfair revocation of my credit card.

My credit limit, and my balance, are relatively small by any standard of comparison. But my credit history is very important to me, and I don't wish to have it marred. Will you please consider reinstating my account, and notify me as soon as possible about your decision? I know that my business may be insignificant in comparison with some customers, but I am basically a creditworthy person, and would like another chance to prove it.

I have enclosed all communication I have received from you and photocopies of cancelled checks for your information.

Thank you very much for your consideration.

Very truly yours,

Lucy Monet

NOTE: the bank reinstated her credit card account shortly thereafter.

Chapter Seven

Credit for

Special

People

EQUAL RIGHTS TO CREDIT EXIST IN THEORY THROUGHOUT THE entire country today. But it doesn't automatically happen if you just stand still. Equal rights are not like rain: it doesn't fall on you. You have to reach out and make yourself equal by helping yourself.

In pursuit of credit, many people find themselves in special situations that often impede their ability to go forward. While not all, and possibly none, of these conditions might apply to you, it's a safe bet that you know someone who would benefit from the following strategies.

STUDENTS AND YOUNG ADULTS:
THE CREDIT ROOKIES

"Youth is wasted on the young" might typify the circumspection felt by many—but not all—creditors. If you have not yet proven yourself, many creditors have the attitude of, "We'll be damned if we'll be your guinea pig." This is the "Catch-22" of credit—you have to have it to get it. However, there are some notable exceptions, as well as a growing recognition of the latent value in retaining the business and consequent loyalty of young consumers between 18 and 30 years old.

Being creditworthy is at least as important as having a high school or even a college degree. And, perhaps surprisingly, credit is easier to get during college than at any other time. Yet the same students who so carefully prepare themselves academically to enter the "working world" often fall miserably short when it comes to developing an elementary knowledge about credit.

During my many visits to college campuses all over the country to lecture and discuss with students the ways and whys of credit, I have found a great gulf of vital information missing in these otherwise well-educated bodies. It seems there are still two things that they don't teach us in school: sex and credit.

Anyway, the misinformation about credit that persists ranges from the comical to the downright dangerous. From a debutante in Dallas: "Whenever I want something, I ask my Daddy. Can't he get me good credit?" From a pre-med student at Ann Arbor: "I'm going to be a doctor. Since doctors are the highest paid professionals on average, I can't imagine how I could have better credit than that. Isn't that so?" The answer to both questions is, of course, NO! It doesn't matter if your papa is the king of Prussia; and M.D. can stand for "Miserable Debtor." Your occupation, who your parents are, have nothing to do with your willingness to pay, a characteristic more telling perhaps than mere ability to repay. Often, very wealthy kids develop the worst habits regarding their personal finances; after all, it's only money to them.

Students should make every effort to establish a positive credit record while they are still in college in order to help ensure their future security. It isn't long after commencement that the graduate begins thinking about making major purchases like a new car or a house. If you don't already have credit at this point, it's extremely difficult to qualify instantly for a sizable car loan or mortgage. And, as we have said before, you may suddenly need credit for an emergency medical or repair bill. Most young adults do not bother to plan ahead for these and other contingencies, and it is often too late to try to begin establishing your credit when you need it in a hurry.

Nearly every college town that I have lectured in has at least one department store that caters to college students in part and offers special introductory lines of credit to students who apply. The amount of credit is relatively modest—usually ranging from $50 to $300—but these stores grant you entrée to that continuing life report card: the credit bureau profile. The requirements for credit acceptance are minimal, but it is still a good idea to make an appeal in person for the store credit card. Your eyes should be clear and your demeanor polite. Creditors may be put out by punksters: if you have purple hair, you might do better applying by mail. And if you subsequently abuse your credit by not paying promptly, creditors are apt to pull the plug on you quickly and reject you when you reapply next semester. They don't take it like a champ; beneath the veneer of civic goodwill lies a strictly dollars-and-sense business ethic.

Another great source for credit is American Express. They offer their green card to college seniors who have no adverse credit history and a promise of a job upon graduation paying $10,000. While American Express is a pay-as-you-go charge card that requires you to pay your bill in full every billing period, it is an important credit reference for other credit grantors.

COLLEGE LOANS

The Reagan administration is doing its best to slash college financial aid programs supported by the federal government. Effective October 1, 1981, tight restrictions were placed on the 9 percent interest, repayable-after-graduation loans. Families with adjusted gross incomes over $30,000 probably no longer qualify unless they have several kids in school at the same time. The yearly limit is $2,500 for undergraduates, $5,000 for graduate students. Yet it has been proposed to no longer accept grad students and to charge a 10 percent origination fee.

The subsequent cuts in subsidized federal loans and grants have wreaked such havoc on so many families unable to find replacement financing that there is certain to be strong congressional pressure to reinstitute part or most of the lost funding. To date, the alternative government college financial aid programs are nothing less than a cruel hoax. It is prophetic that one of the only new programs meant to repair some of the damage done to students is called ALAS—Auxiliary Loans to Assist Students. But the terms are so stingy that we hesitate to recommend signing up for it: a fixed 14 percent loan up to $3,000 per year, with repayment starting 60 days after the loan is granted. You have five to 10 years to repay, but only 14 states have enacted banking legislation so far allowing the federal program to be tapped.

Another federal program for medical students called HEAL is even more abhorrent. Terms have been as high as 20 percent per year for a minimum of 10 years, and there are no allowances for prepayment. A $20,000 loan under this program—$5,000 per year—amounts to a $100,000 obligation. This is outright usury and it is scandalous for the U.S. government to pose as a shill for the banking industry. Don't accept these terms no matter how much pressure the financial aid office brings to bear.

Virtually all the other grant and loan programs have been hit as well, including Pell grants, the Supplemental Education Opportunity Grant Program, the National Direct Student Loan Program (5 percent loans to undergraduate and grad students based on demonstrated need), and matching programs with state student incentive grants.

A pathetic part of the barren landscape are many of the college financial aid offices. Squeezed by both the shrinking pool of funds while the costs for college continue to balloon at more than 10 percent per year for the last five years, financial aid officers are charged with the impossible task of doing more with less. They are under siege. Desperate students, parents, and alumni often vent their rage at their inability to set things right.

Most financial aid officers are no doubt performing a tough task well, guiding worried students and parents through the maze of forms and eligibility provisions. As an applicant for grants and/or loans, whatever the source, you should be prepared for one of the most tedious, protracted and exasperating experiences. Your financial aid officer is not your adversary in this process; make sure you accord to him or her the same type of respect and diligence we talked about in the interview chapter. A good financial aid officer knows about more than just how to help you fill out the forms. A plethora of grants and scholarships still operate under all sorts of governances. You can buy all sorts of guides (and they are sometimes very helpful), but there is no substitute for a true professional who keeps up with the continual changes in the field.

Once again, your job is to separate yourself from the screaming masses. Once you have been accepted and have decided which college you will attend, try to schedule a personal appointment with a financial aid officer on campus. The late spring and summer months are generally less hectic times and hence more appropriate for arranging such a meeting. If you live within a day's drive of campus, there should be no question that this investment in time will be worthwhile. And you should consider such a meeting as a long-term investment—don't expect to walk out of the office with a commitment for money in hand.

POSITIONING YOURSELF FOR AID
The way to increase your potential eligibility for higher education financial aid is precisely the opposite of how you demonstrate your creditworthiness, with one exception.

Oddly enough, however, receiving financial aid can and should be used as an additional qualification of your credit worth. The one exception naturally is your character, or willingness to repay.

While creditors want to see sizable capacity (income) and collateral (any other assets) in order for you to qualify for most loans, you have to downplay the value of these two factors to be eligible for many grants, scholarships, and certain subsidized loans. How do you do this? The most important thing to do is to plan your strategy as far ahead as possible. Many options are already closed to you by the time you get around to applying for school. Parents should talk with their accountants about the ramifications of setting up separate accounts for their children in anticipation of paying college costs. Sure you can reduce your own taxes on interest income that way, but when it comes time to ask for financial aid, the college first assumes that you will totally clean out your kid's account and use it to pay its bill. It cannot make that same assumption with the money in the parents' account. One option may be to move that nest egg into an account of one of the parents just before the aid application is submitted.

An early start will also allow you to search for many sources of scholarships and loans. You might begin by asking your high school guidance office what funds are being made available within your community. And don't wait until you or your son or daughter is in the tenth or eleventh grade. Many local clubs, civic groups, and fraternal organizations that make awards for higher education favor applicants, either officially or just by nature, who have someone in their family who has been active in the group for a number of years. Make sure the application and you are not presumptuous in your supposed "right" to an award. Arrogance is seldom rewarded.

Other sources of private aid are published in a growing variety of reference books on the subject. A few worth mentioning include *Financial Aids for Higher Education*, which lists more than 5,000 sources and is available in many public libraries; *Need a Lift?*, which costs $1.00 from the American Legion Education Program (Box 1055, Indianapolis, Ind. 46206); and *Don't Miss Out* by Robert Leider, $2.50 from Octameron Press, P.O. Box 3437, Alexandria, Va. 22302.

Other ways to position your family to become eligible for financial aid may include placing your savings in tax-deferred annuities that do not count as part of your calculated assets; investing in "tax shelters" to reduce current income; and declaring the value of your home as low as possible (it doesn't have to coincide strictly with what you believe is the true market value). Again, an accountant should be consulted to make sure that one or more of these methods are right for you.

One trick that many parents took advantage of was to enroll in a local college class or two themselves, thereby increasing the number of students in the household, and consequently qualifying for loans they may not have been eligible for otherwise. The College Scholarship Service, a subsidiary of the College Board, which processes financial aid applications for many of the thousands of colleges and universities around the country, plans to recommend excluding parents from eligibility calculations. However, if you can substantiate that these courses are necessary as part of a continuing education related to your job or even as a requisite transition in order for you to change careers, you should appeal this arbitrary decision. Attach a supplement to the CSS application form that substantiates how vital these courses are to your career. If your employer is amenable, include a short note from your boss verifying this fact. And follow up with the college of your choice to make sure that they are aware of your special need.

Speaking of employers, if your family income threatens to increase above the maximum eligibility level for the 9 percent guaranteed student loan program, perhaps you can agree to strike a deal. Instead of increasing your salary, maybe your company allows for accelerating the appreciation of your pension, or agreeing to assume your charitable contributions for the year, or any number of other "perks," like club memberships that can be drawn so that they do not have to be stated as part of your income.

All this requires careful planning: the financial aid people typically want last year's income tax statement to corroborate your application, so last-minute changes in how you are remunerated for your work might show up too late to sway them.

A new type of counselor has cropped up all across the country to meet this increased need of finding ways to pay for tuition—for a nice fee. They call themselves "student aid agencies," student consulting services, or specialized private financial counselors. Some use microcomputers to store and code financial aid sources and claim to match the student applicants with aid for which they qualify for a fee that ranges from $45 to $250 and even more. Many engage in deceptive advertising, promising a computer printout of "Funds worth up to $10,000 to $20,000 or more, for which you qualify." In fact, most of their clients end up receiving no aid at all, and are out the service fee besides. Stay away from these hucksters; most prey on fear and desperation. And if you think a bit and spend a little time on research, you can do a better job than any third party.

Some financial aid offices are not weathering the deluge of requests well. They are not taking it like champs at all. Seriously, we have encountered a number of financial aid offices that refuse to grant personal interviews. Others do not acknowledge their mail or bother to correspond beyond form letters. This will not do: financial aid officers have a professional responsibility to their customers, no matter how taxing this becomes at times. Campus administrations in their zeal to economize must learn to distinguish between the acceptable levels of mechanization in registering for classes and the special personal requirements involved in aiding students to finance their higher education. Shabbily treated students will not make for very generous alumni.

Lousy service should be brought to the attention of administrators and heads of alumni groups.

If and when all of these sources happen to fall short, consider approaching a relative or a friend for a loan. He or she might agree to terms unheard of in today's market. The details will be delineated further in the next chapter.

BLACKS AND OTHER MINORITIES

Blacks and Hispanics and other minorities in different parts of the country have suffered through all sorts of discrimination, including the capricious denial of credit. Of course, there are federal laws prohibiting credit discrimination on the basis of race, creed, religion, sex, and age, but certain past practices continue to plague you.

For instance, even after it became illegal to discriminate against credit applicants because of their race, a major New York bank continued to code black applications for loans with a "V.E." at the bottom of the form. If the black inquired as to what that meant, he or she was told, "Verify Employment. It's just an instruction to the credit department." In truth, it was a tipoff that the applicant was black.

Even today, blacks and other minorities have to be a little more diligent in filling out their applications for credit. Because most, if not all, banks continue to use a judgmental system of scoring credit applications, they are free to interpret the facts. Veracity can suddenly become an overriding concern; if your stated length of residence or employment or your salary proves to be exaggerated when they run a check on your application, you can be branded a liar—suspect, not worthy of credit. Never mind that creditors often routinely assume that all applications are padded to some extent. If they know you are a minority, bankers are more likely to become more diligent in reviewing your claims, seeking some aberration to hang their hat on—and cut off your chance for credit. This is the new form of "redlining." Since, by law, banks are no longer allowed to deny credit (traditionally, mortgages) because the area or zip code is deemed undesirable, they now often go to greater legal lengths to find other faults with your application or credit history.

Of course, none of this is admitted by the banks or other large creditors. Their advertising agencies are careful to include the obligatory black and other minorities as well as to place the "Equal Opportunity Lender" indicia on the bottom of their commercials and print campaigns. While this represents a welcome boon to some minority actors, these cosmetic touches cannot cover up the plain fact that many large commercial banks are actively trying to shed their so-called marginal accounts, and that a large percentage of blacks and other minorities fall into this category.

So why knock yourself out trying to appease a decidedly unappreciative banker? Why not stick with or retreat to the traditional and friendly lender of lower income blacks and other minorities—the personal finance companies? Many, in fact, are minority owned. There are two reasons.

First, you are paying an exorbitantly high price for borrowing money, usually over 30 percent and often more than 40 percent. A $300 TV ends up costing you over $1,000 by the time you're through making payments. Sure, the payments are made easy for you: a collector comes to you every week, most likely payday, to pick up the $10 or $20 from you, and then you're free and clear—at least until next payday. The trouble is the light weekly burden masks the truly oppressive cumulative weight you ultimately shoulder. You have to think about your opportunity costs. What could you have done with all that extra cash had it not gone to fancy financing? Look long and hard at the expensive, new automobile your bill collector arrives in next time you're due. You helped pay for it, $10 or $20 at a clip. Sure, you build up your credit standing with a personal finance company, just like any other creditor, but by the time you're out from under those seemingly endless weekly payments, what is it that you own? How much is it worth now, two, three, four, five years later? And how long will it be before it breaks down and you'll have to start all over again with nothing to show for it?

Second, many commercial banks look askance at a credit history that includes dealing with a personal finance company, no matter how successfully you completed your repayment schedule. Not only doesn't it count for you—it's a negative factor. Why? Experience. A credit official at Bank of America privately conceded that an analysis of problem loans (both delinquent and defaults) revealed that an extraordinary percentage of its customers who had prior dealings with private consumer finance companies ran into trouble with bank loans. They also happened to be black. The credit department then had to wrestle with the problem of deciding whether making this a negative element of its scoring system was a valid criterion or just thinly veiled racism. The formal decision was not made known to us, but in formal and informal training of consumer-oriented bankers, a word of caution goes out regarding new credit customers with personal finance loan histories.

The banks' bad experience with debtors who have dealt with personal finance companies in the past may have something to do with the collection process. With many of these community-based personal finance companies, the collector comes to you. Week after week, the onus is put on the creditor to show up, even find you, if necessary. Sometimes this leads to little games of hide-and-seek. And they come to expect this: their costs are built right into your sky-high interest rates. What you learn about trust from these personal finance companies is not only negligible but damaging in terms of developing a true sense of what the concept really means. They don't trust you. They come after you and if you don't have the money, they'll come back and take away the furniture, or whatever it is that you bought on time. Not right away, mind you—after all, they are making good money off of you, even if you fall behind a couple of weeks—but they will collect what is their fair due. This short-leash approach to financing amounts to a quasi-instant collection agency. And there's precious little trust built in that environment (see Chapter 10).

It is important for blacks and other minorities to avail themselves of the lower priced services of certain sectors of the banking or financial services industry. Although many large commercial banks are turning their backs on moderate and lower income customers, there are still many smaller commercial banks eager for this business. Just as important to consider are credit unions, savings and loan associations, and mutual savings banks. (They are discussed at greater length in the next chapter.)

Whatever your choice, you must be vigilant so that certain stereotypes do not cloud your credit prospects. On the reverse side of a loan application or on a separate worksheet, a creditor will make certain assumptions about your budget, or spending habits. Many whites hold the view that blacks tend to spend more on consumer goods and save less than whites with comparable income. In fact, just the opposite is true, according to a report cited in *Forbes* magazine and prepared for the University of Michigan in 1981 by Marcus Alexis, a member of the Interstate Commerce Commission; George Haines of the University of Toronto; and Leonard Simon, a Rochester, New York, banker. Beyond generally saving more and spending less, they found that blacks specifically spend less for housing, medical care, and car travel, while spending more on clothing and nonautomobile transportation than comparable whites. No consistent differences in spending on home furnishings and equipment, recreation, or leisure were found between blacks and whites of like income. And in terms of food spending, blacks who make their purchases at small, inner-city grocery stores pay higher prices than suburbanites who patronize supermarkets.

Do not wait to be miscast in such an assumed budget. Draw up your own and be prepared to defend it, citing this report if need be. It must, of course, be within reason; you have prepared it for yourself as much as for any creditor, and you must expect to abide by it.

Blacks and other disadvantaged minorities admittedly will have to work harder to be granted the credit that is their due. The importance of submitting your own budget showing a 10 to 15 percent surplus beyond the cost of financing your proposed debt cannot be stressed enough. Creditors are bowled over by this demonstration of caring. Your composure, delineated in the interview chapter, can also make the difference between acceptance and rejection.

Some years ago, a black real estate entrepreneur approached a banking associate of mine for a potpourri of loans. Near the end of the dialogue, the entrepreneur was alleged to have asked, "Is it a problem for you that I'm black?" My normally taciturn cohort literally all but gave him the bank.

The lack of a credit profile should not be detrimental. Your reply is, "That is, in part, why I have chosen you as my first reporting creditor."

NEWLY MOVED AND INTERMITTENTLY UNEMPLOYED

We have lumped these two seemingly incongruous groups because of their mutual concern for timing. The rule here is: Go for credit when you are most stable—*before* you move and *while* you still have a job. Both require planning.

The average American now makes 14 changes of address during his or her lifetime. It should not be traumatic to your creditors and your credit need not be affected. However, it is easy to get hurt if you don't take the initiative. First, consider carefully whether you truly expect your move out of state or to a distant community to be permanent. If your company is transferring you for a two- or three-year assignment, it's probably wise to maintain your banking relationship at a reduced level rather than closing it entirely. Meet with your banker and explain that you fully intend to return, that your relationship with the bank is important to you and you want to keep it open while you are away. Do not be swayed by a banker who says, "Well, it's no problem opening a new account when you return." Just make sure that your savings and/or checking accounts are above the minimum level for free or nominal service charges.

Next, ask for a letter of reference from your banker stating: (1) the number of years you have maintained accounts at the bank, including other members of your family; (2) any line of credit that the bank allowed you, whether used or not (if used, the successful repayment of that line of credit); (3) any other service that you used during the years—from traveler's checks to a safe-deposit box; and (4) any general statement as to your character.

Your banker may be slightly put out by this request; it's not in line with what he or she is used to. Assure the banker that you realize that it is not a standard request but that you are concerned about maintaining your credit standing in your new locale. You *need* your bank's good recommendation: persist. If the banker seems at a loss, have your request in writing and say you'll leave it with him or her and call back later. This is only a last resort if you believe that the person you are chatting with does not feel he or she has the responsibility or authority to comply with your request.

This is also a good time to check your credit profile to make sure that the information on file is accurate. Fix any mistakes, as outlined in Chapter 2. Also, get similar letters of reference from other creditors who have not reported to the credit bureau.

Beyond that, review all of your credit cards. Cards from department stores that are not located where you are moving should be destroyed, with notification, if you have no intention of using them again; or, better yet, wherever you have a predetermined cash maximum, keep them but ask the store to reduce your credit limit to the minimum. Actually, your smartest move is to ask the department store's credit department if the parent company has another department store company in the area to which you are moving. Then ask what is the simplest way for your credit history and line of credit to be transferred. For instance,

Bloomingdale's in New York is owned by Federated Department Stores, which also owns Filene's in Boston, among other stores.

National credit cards can be easily transferred to your new address by simply notifying the department store by mail with your payment. Make sure you plaster the notification several times on the form so that the clerks take note. Better yet, staple your check to your new address.

If you have already moved, these same accommodations can be made, but at much greater effort. You are a relatively unknown quantity, but try to get your past to follow you into your new present, selectively if at all possible.

Many self-employed and seasonally employed people go through periods of unemployment, making it more difficult to develop a solid credit standing. As we have said, stability is symptomatic of good credit. While you are working, you should arrange to meet with your banker and acknowledge that your career is subject to intermittent periods of unemployment or underemployment. However, on balance, you have to dramatize the factors that demonstrate what stability you have accomplished—that is, the length of time in your profession, the number of years living at the same residence, and the length of time you have managed to successfully fulfill your credit obligations. Certainly this is some measure of creditworthiness, and most bankers will acknowledge it.

Any application for credit cannot ask you whether you anticipate losing your job, so you are protected from the prying of suspicious creditors. But be sure to apply well before any current job is finished. Do not make any false promises or lie about having other work lined up. This will only diminish your creditworthiness if it doesn't come to pass.

Applying for credit while you are unemployed is just about hopeless for all but the most frivolous forms of credit, unless you can demonstrate other income streams. Perhaps other members of your household are bringing in some money. What must be demonstrated beyond who is employed is that cash is coming in and that there is a good likelihood that it will continue to do so. This can be done better in person, as we have said; waving a passbook in someone's face is much more credible than just leaving the salary side blank on your credit application and mysteriously entering respectable numbers under "other income."

Do not be suckered into paying classified ad con artists for worthless information about oodles of credit supposedly available to anyone whether or not he or she has a job. Some make promises of MasterCard or VISA to anyone for a hefty professional fee. Don't you go for that. Does money grow on trees? Just because your newspaper may have no scruples about who it makes its money from does not mean you should be bamboozled. Every so often, enough people complain and the district attorneys have to get to work.

WOMEN

A woman should always have money and credit of her own. No matter what your status or lifestyle, money and credit are essential to cope with an unknown future and, perhaps more importantly, to improve and ensure your current state of well-being. In scores of conversations with bankers, credit industry officials, lawyers, and other credit experts, they all mouthed the importance of women actively establishing their own credit, notwithstanding the guarantees of the Equal Credit Opportunity Act. Most agreed that women still have a lot of catching up to do in terms of creating credit but attributed this to a lack of knowledge and/or initiative rather than to any impediments along the path, legal or otherwise.

Whatever the causes, the facts are that women generally display a higher reliability in repaying their debts. Various academic studies, including several done under the auspices of the Consumer Credit Center at Purdue University, attest to women's higher reliability in regard to debt repayment. Yet this better reliability has not yet come close to being recognized by greater creditworthiness. Until October of 1975—less than a decade ago—women were routinely manipulated and scorned by creditors, however unwittingly these practices supposedly evolved. Many women who had never bothered to build their own credit histories—or were discouraged from doing so—were effectively locked out of the credit market. The family unit was embodied by the man and there was thought to be little need to involve the wife, except to make sure that the checks were signed. Whether you are single, married, separated, divorced, or widowed, stories still abound of the lives limited or damaged by less-than-scrupulous lenders:

- Edith B., widow, had her despair compounded by the elimination of her family's credit standing when her husband died.
- Anna G., working, divorced mother, had her credit application rejected because her former husband was considered a deadbeat.
- Joan R., single, couldn't get a department store credit card even though she had no debts and a steady job.
- Kelly S., career executive, earning a good salary, was told to get her husband's signature on her small loan application.

These arbitrary credit abuses are now, for the most part, illegal. Through the passage of local, state, and federal laws prohibiting credit discrimination on account of sex, women today can develop their own credit standing and power. The federal Equal Credit Opportunity Act of 1975 finally evens the score between the sexes—at least in theory. It is a very complicated law which yields in part to the peculiarities of certain state laws, most notably the community property state laws. In addition, some stodgy bankers continue to relate better to male customers or construct their scoring system to favor men, however inadvertently. Be careful, female bankers are sometimes equally culpable. The veritable bottom line remains that just because the law is in place does not guarantee that potential creditors will grant you the assumptions you deserve. Credit continues to be a privilege, and creditors still have a lot of leeway in interpreting the supposed facts. But knowing your rights under the law(s) and exercising them where need be should form an integral part of your overall strategy aimed at getting all the credit you deserve. Again, you have to reach out.

The Right Name

In America, when a woman marries, she more often than not adopts her husband's surname as her own. The trend in recent years, however, has been away from this, especially among better-educated women. While many men may privately mourn the dissipation of this tradition, it seems rather unreasonable for a woman to give up her own identity. Nevertheless, a woman has to decide among a number of possible legal names upon marriage. What is most important to realize is that in order for your credit to follow you properly, you should be consistent in the name you choose. When Deborah Jane Jones marries Sydney Carton, she has five choices for a name: (1) she can keep her maiden name—Deborah J. Jones; (2) she can take his last name without dropping any of her names—Deborah J. Jones Carton; (3) she can take his last name with her maiden name serving as a middle name—Deborah Jones Carton; (4) She can drop her maiden surname and take his—Deborah Jane Carton; or (5) she can drop both her maiden surname and middle name and take his surname—Deborah Carton.

For proper identification purposes—especially if your last name is fairly common—it is wise always to have three names or at least a middle initial handy. An unacceptable and not legally binding name on any credit application is Mrs. Sydney Carton. That is merely a social title and could be held by a succession of women.

What's in a name? Plenty, if you're smart. Reserve for yourself the best of both worlds—keep your name and only take his if there is fiscal opportunity.

Sole Versus Joint Accounts

The first usual step to establishing your financial identity is to open a checking and savings account in your own name. A joint checking account may be enough only if it has a line of credit and if your partner is not in the habit of bouncing checks. Since 1977, all information on any type of joint credit accounts (ordinary checking accounts don't count)—be they credit cards, charge cards, or personal loans—must be filed under both parties' individual credit bureau profiles, if that particular creditor reports it.

For all the conveniences of joint accounts, the one drawback is that they are not truly a measure of your sole creditworthiness. Potential creditors are hard pressed to figure out who was responsible for what.

On any application, list only your income if you don't want it to wind up as a joint account. Among your sources of income, creditors must accept alimony payments as a legitimate source. However, you do not have to make any mention of alimony if you believe your other income is sufficient. Many creditors are asking more detailed questions about alimony on their applications because of the unfortunately frequent irregularity of payments and other disputes instigated by incorrigible ex-husbands.

It is best for both parties involved in a divorce to make an effort to portray an amicable facade at least for current and future creditors. Many potential creditors get nervous and want to know more than they are entitled to in their zeal to minimize risk. If you can agree to provide each other with soothing statements without letting lawyers rile you into nonproductive antagonisms, your credit standing faces a better chance of remaining intact.

Credit Survival Agreement

> It is mutually agreed that upon dissolution of our marriage, we will each maintain separate ownership of our credit as if it were an item of property. Each party

agrees to do nothing to impinge upon the integrity of each other's credit.

(Agreed, signed, and dated)

Career Woman

In 1981, there were 16.2 million women living on their own, with no husband and no children under age 18, according to the Current Population Survey, Bureau of the Census. The American Council of Life Insurance reports that during the first 70 years of this century the number of years a woman worked outside of the home on the average rose from only six years to 23 years. Within the last decade, the increase continued dramatically. Why is this worth mentioning? Because this development has not gone unnoticed by the business community, including the credit industry. In part due to provisions of the Equal Credit Opportunity Act and largely because it is supported in fact, career women are finally being granted their just rewards as far as credit is concerned. Still, problems persist.

Among working women who are single and in childbearing years, some creditors make a distinction between women without educational training. The theory is that women who commit themselves to the requisite education in order to enter into a professional field generally view their work as a career. The positive implications of such a view are that creditors are apt to recognize this marketability and assign credit without worrying about the possible interruption of employment because of childbearing. In fact, many women who leave the work force to have children are increasingly able to resume their careers with their same or another employer within six months.

Those who remain susceptible to less than adequate levels of credit are working, single women of childbearing age who are not professionals or who are not employed in jobs considered as requiring specialized skills. Creditors fear a retreat to the home or other symptoms of "burnout" even though these prejudices are illegal. Women in this position should consider the following supplements to their loan or credit application: (1) elaborate on your job with a description of your duties, detailing in some fashion the importance or the unique skills acquired that either make you important in the overall operations of the company or that can readily be transferred to another employer; (2) certify your acknowledged value by citing your frequency of advancement, bonuses, or other company citations. Include the pat on the back for a job well done—just ask your boss if he or she would be kind enough to put it in writing so that you can use it to improve your credit rating.

The Job Stability Reference

Your employer generally can be a valuable source for creating and continuing your creditworthiness. A lender's interest in your stability of employment is often just a means of groping for a way to measure your job security. If you can appease potential creditors by providing them with a recent written report regarding your good standing in said company, you can rebuke the normal qualms and throw their scoring models out the window.

The importance of framing your request properly for a stability reference from your boss cannot be emphasized enough. It is an admittedly novel proposal. Most employers should be sympathetic if you present yourself in a calm yet earnest fashion. First, assure your superior that you are not in any personal trouble, but that you would appreciate his or her help. Explain your interest in being granted credit and say that you have reason to believe that you might encounter some resistance due to the creditor's inability to gauge your job security properly. Make sure you plug your unstinting commitment to the company at this time. Let it be known that you have no interest in using the letter in any other manner beyond showing it to your creditor(s). Explain that it must be in writing in order to maximize its effectiveness because you cannot rely on the creditor's diligence in contacting your employer by phone beyond verifying your employment. Creditors seldom ask whether an applicant is an employee in good standing, let alone whether the company has an active interest in retaining and grooming the applicant for further responsibilities in the future.

If your boss is extremely busy or you think he or she might not have the time or inclination to compose a special letter, you might want to present a typewritten specimen as a model to be transferred onto his or her stationery. However, you could be surprised by a much more complimentary testimonial if you leave your boss the chore of creating the reference. Use your judgment. Here's a sample:

> *To Whom It May Concern:*
>
> *Deborah J. Carton has proven herself to be a valuable asset to the XYZ Corporation. In only (state period of employment), our investment in training her in the research and development division has been rewarded by a most productive and profitable grasp of her duties. In fact, we have every intention and hope of retaining Ms. Carton for additional responsibilities and future advancement.*
>
> *(Signed with title and date)*

Don't let your boss react with an "I'm sorry, but if I did this for you, I'd have to write a letter for everyone employed under me and I wouldn't be able to get my job done. If Personnel can't help you, I'm sorry." Cut off the escape hatch by stressing that you consider this to be a confidential request that will continue to remain in your confidence. Acknowledge that you realize your request is outside the range of his or her normal duties and responsibilities, but that this help would be a great service in cutting through a lot of possible encumbrances.

A good time to make this proposal is during a private conference for a performance or salary review. Who knows, you might even convince your boss that the idea would be worth popping on his or her own superior.

A totally unacceptable line of questioning some creditors used to employ concerned birth control practices and childbearing plans. This is now illegal, as is the use of any statistical tables to predict the likelihood that you will have children in the future. If a creditor asks you orally about these issues, state that this approach is illegal.

As is the case with anyone else, you are allowed to include in your income stream any part-time jobs, pensions, social security, other investments, or public assistance programs. Alimony payments must be considered a legitimate source of income, but you need not report it on a credit application unless you feel it would help prove that your income is sufficient to meet your proposed payment schedule or credit exposure.

Career women should have relatively little difficulty obtaining and maintaining credit to the extent that debts are kept in line and income keeps pace with the cost of living. The lack of dependents is a definite plus and, in general, you are qualified to be granted every advancement in credit as long as you meet each new obligation.

Homemakers

Married women without paying jobs traditionally have an extremely difficult time qualifying for their own credit. If all of the money is coming in from the husband's efforts, he should be the one signing for any request for credit, according to conventional wisdom. Applying for joint credit can help: since 1977, joint accounts that are reported to credit bureaus must automatically contribute to each spouse's individual credit file. Still, an unemployed debtor without a proven income stream does not have very convincing credit credentials.

What to do? Your options are admittedly limited, but if you are serious about creating, maintaining, and improving your separate credit capacity, there are a couple of options to consider.

First, before getting married, every woman should independently and carefully think about what to do with her accumulated savings and other assets, including anticipated cash gifts from parents or other relatives. Too many women automatically kick in everything they have into a common pool or joint account. It may sound crass and unmagnanimous to suggest an objective evaluation of protecting your financial needs in marriage, especially if you plan to stop working in a paying job. After all, marriage is an adventure in faith, love, and devotion, a union for better or for worse. However, the sad statistics are showing that more, if not most, starts are proving to be false. We are not necessarily advocating that you enter the holy state of matrimony with less than total commitment, but that commitment should not be confused with consignment. All women, but especially the woman who foregoes a career because of marriage should think about retaining her financial assets as a separate income-producing vehicle. While it may be said that the employed husband assumes a greater or unfair share of the financial burden under this arrangement, many couples realize that a strict dollar accounting method for apportioning the family budget short-shrifts the unemployed spouse, who cannot replace her depleted funds. In other words, is it really fair for the husband to ask his wife to put up the $20,000 she saved or got from her parents even if he is contributing an equal or greater amount for the down payment on a house? He can go out and get more where that came from. She has agreed not to in order to raise a family, and is further deprived of the income that that nest-egg produced. Her ownership or equity position in the house is not liquid and cannot be used on a credit application as a source of income with which to pay back a loan.

The point is that a heart-to-heart discussion of long-term finances before you get married is often necessary and realistic in order to quell or clarify any potential misunderstandings or wrong assumptions. If you agree that you want to raise a family, requiring you to be out of work for a considerable span of years, it might be wise to limit or prorate your cash contribution to the marriage and invest your money separately to provide continued income through your underemployed years. In this way, you can preserve and build upon your own credit, let alone your psychic sense of well-being.

Another partial solution that a number of canny wives have worked out with their husbands is to monetize the value of their housework. In other words, you figure out the market price of all the chores done around the house, including childrearing. Check the classified ads to find out the current salaries for housekeepers and governesses. Again, many life insurance companies provide these figures in order to sell homemaker life insurance policies.

Talk it over with your husband. Most routinely hand over the paycheck to be deposited into joint checking and other accounts to cover the bills. Instead, you could suggest that he in effect "employ" you by paying out a percentage of his check on a regular basis to be put into your own personal account. In turn, you could agree to pay for some of the household expenses out of this fund. Just make sure that you are consistent in paying the same bills and allocate enough for a reasonable surplus. The formula for determining what your are entitled to depends upon your husband's income and how much credit you want and reasonably need. Certainly, you should not expect the same "salary" whether your husband is a clerk making $17,000 or a doctor making $117,000. The greater the funds available, the more likely you can persuade your husband that you are entitled to a direct payment of your housework services, probably around $20,000 a year. In circumstances where that figure or another that you choose exceeds 50 percent of his income, you might suggest that you split it in half. If you live in a community property state, you are legally entitled to half, no matter what the spouse's income, in that you are also considered co-owner of all income and assets acquired during the marriage, as well as debts.

Caution: Don't get cute and try to quantify love and affection. And remember that money is an extremely emotional issue. Many psychologists claim that conflicts over money contribute to or are central to the dissolution of most marriages today. This may not be a practical or realistic proposal for all housewives, or househusbands, for that matter. The simple underriding premise is that because you are contributing to your family's standard of living, you believe that it is in both of your interests to acquire your own credit standing. Look at it this way: it's another safety valve. If your spouse screws up his own credit or a joint account, there is another source to tap in the event of an emergency.

After a few months under this new arrangement, apply for credit *in person* along with your completed application. Under the occupation question, write in "Self-employed." Bring along your bank passbook and checking account, as well as at least one letter from a creditor who was previously being paid out of joint account who currently is receiving payment from you alone. Follow the guidelines in the interview chapter and be sure to state that the reason you are applying for credit, besides an interest in the service, is a desire to start and upgrade your credit standing. Offer to start out with a relatively low credit limit at first in order to prove yourself. Ask what the minimum line of credit is, and agree that this is fine for the time being. Stress that the important thing is being given a chance to prove your good name by the bank's good name and to have it recorded.

If your income, as such, is still considered insufficient, a potential credit grantor has the right to require you to find a suitable cosigner. But the creditor cannot stipulate that the cosigner be your husband necessarily. In fact, you might be in a stronger position to extricate yourself and your cosigner from such a bond if that creditworthy person is *not* your husband. After six months or a year of successful debt repayment, another personal meeting with your creditor might result in relieving that someone from the role of continued cosignership. Cosigning with your husband, on the other hand, amounts to a joint account and is apt to remain so indefinitely.

Working Women in Two-Income Households

Among 56 percent of married couples, both are gainfully employed. The Life Insurance Marketing and Research Association recently conducted a survey that showed that in one third of the households where both partners are working, the wife's income was equal to or greater than the husband's. Creditors are no fools; naturally, they prefer lending money to those people who already have money. So it should come as no surprise that this recent development of a surge in dual-income households has creditors all abuzz in marketing ploys to get a piece of your action. You're a desirable commodity. You can't help but see the upbeat commercials on television of upscale couples who ooze insouciance while consuming credit conspicuously. These purveyors of plastic are supposed to be desirable role models. Fetching female models abound, sneering or gloating over their credit clout. It's all very slick and seductive to many men and women alike. And it works. What the commercials don't show, however, are the unhappy masses of boys and girls who for one reason or another don't make the credit cut and are condemned to another season in the minor leagues of life.

Stick to your sums when applying for your own credit. And remember that credit is a business, like any business, interested in profitable expansion. So while by law a creditor cannot ask you for your husband's income, occupation, or any other data concerning him when you apply for your own credit, be aware that a credit employee sometimes changes hats and acts as a marketing person as well during personal interviews. Often, the employee is instructed to try and convert a single account into a joint account to expand the creditor's customer base. Typical strategies include stressing the convenience inherent in a dual account. Or perhaps a lovely new men's department in the traditionally women's oriented store. It doesn't wash: commingling credit will inevitably cause perceptual problems for other creditors down the line.

When applying for a closed-end or installment loan, you should be sure to submit with your application a supplemental budget worksheet that shows your level of financial contribution to the family budget. Follow the instructions in the application chapter and be sure to show a bottom-line surplus of 10 percent beyond the cost of carrying the loan. During the interview, a crafty banker may try to recast your application with words to the effect of, "Well, your budget shows me that you are really applying for a family loan, which should be a shared obligation." The banker will stop short of asking you to bring in your husband as a co-signer, but will leave the door wide open in the discussion, hoping you will volunteer his participation. If and when these tactics are subtly introduced, you can either confront or deflect the issue.

Confrontations are best avoided under all but the most trying of circumstances. As a rule, you don't make any points telling a person where to get off, no matter how slimy the person is or how righteous you feel. The one exception may be when a person thinks you are a simpleton and is trying to hoodwink you into a decidedly dumb proposition, like signing your husband up for credit when you are creditworthy in your own right. If you feel that there is some hesitation on the part of the potential credit grantor because you have too little credit experience, go back to the old reliable retort that you are *determined* to establish your own credit, that this is the most critical aspect of your request, and that you require from a suitable creditor a sensitivity to this legitimate need and a corresponding understanding that, under these circumstances especially, you are not about to come close to being delinquent with the loan. Do not act exasperated: it may be taken as a sign that you have been through the mill before with other potential creditors, whether it's true or you admit to it or not.

As mentioned in the interview chapter, the most suitable way to confront a balky banker or any other credit grantor is to turn the questioning around. Ask him or her point blank eyeball-to-eyeball whether on the face of it you are likely to be granted your request for credit. Creditors are trained to act and speak deferentially to all but the basket credit cases so prod politely, but prod. And if you are not properly reassured that your business is welcome, ask for the application back. *Remember, you have not signed it yet.*

For those less certain of their perceived worth, deflecting the issue of a lack of proven credit experience amounts to a change of venue. What must be done many times is to offer your creditor the opportunity to fiddle around with the terms of the loan, assuming of course that it remains an individual account. Ask: "Would you prefer it if the monthly payments were smaller over a longer period of time? Maybe you would be more comfortable if my credit request were slightly smaller?" You may have to make a decision whether your desire for a specific amount of credit supersedes your interest in immediately creating an independently secure credit profile. Often enough, it is possible to convert at a later date joint obligations and relationships to more precisely acknowledge your own worth.

Single Parents

The Current Population Survey counted 9.1 million women who were the sole heads of their households in 1981, up 65 percent from 1970.

Being a single parent is very tough work, and creditors know it. Women with children but no husband usually earn less than men in the same spot. In general, women still earn only about 60 percent of the median income for men in year-round, full-time jobs. So single mothers not only find themselves in the unenviable position of being totally responsible for the care of their children, they also typically have such small incomes as to make the granting of credit seem implausible. These unfortunate women are often forced to borrow from family and friends—if they are lucky. Otherwise, they may be forced to turn to personal finance companies, pawnbrokers, or, worst of all, loan sharks.

Personal finance companies are traditional lures for people in poor fiscal shape. Their marketing angle has been ease of payments, but they make you pay dearly for it, typically charging the maximum allowable rates by law, which exceed 30 percent in some states. All borrowers, including single parents, should avoid these lenders if at all possible and rely instead on their personal integrity. You may have to reach out for compassion when applying for a loan, but you must still keep your eye on the total nut for the best deal.

Single mothers must take care with their application for closed-end credit. Bankers make assumptions regarding family budgets which often grossly overstate the true costs of carrying the household. For instance, many divorced mothers who retain custody of their children nevertheless grant visitation rights to their ex-husbands on a regular basis. If a former husband in effect pays for the feeding and care of the children every weekend and/or a month or more during the course of the year, these financial obligations diminish the budgetary load. Moreover, alimony must be considered a legitimate form of income. If the ex-in-laws are in the habit of helping out with occasional cash gifts, this should be stated, however conservatively.

For mothers with children under five, try to conserve funds by obtaining child care while you are at work from a trusted relative or neighbor rather than an organized group care facility, which typically costs a great deal more. Sometimes such an arrangement can be struck by suggesting a trade-off of services—whether it be cleaning or bookkeeping. Or perhaps you can convince your employer to let the child accompany you to work.

Whatever your arrangement, be sure to include as part of your supplemental application the fact that you have taken care of a considerable responsibility at less than the bank's normal assumptions for budgeting your expenses. Also, if you can demonstrate flexibility in your work schedule and a convenient workplace location, mention these characteristics as factors contributing to the stability of your job and income.

Another source of credit may be your employer. Is he or she considered understanding, approachable? If so, when you make your appeal use the same methods and diligence detailed in the interview and application chapters. Make sure your employer realizes that you don't just want a loan until the next payday. You are requesting a loan to help stabilize your life and help make you a better employee. Work out the numbers before you make your presentation—it should be a level of debt that you can reasonably handle. In fact, do not assume that you have to accept an interest rate level above the prime commercial lending rate, or even at prime. Take advantage of the fact that you are approaching your employer for an admittedly extraordinary request; under these circumstances, and considering the very high interest rates available through normal commercial channels, your employer might be sympathetic to a fair and reasonable rate. At this writing, a rate of 10 percent might be acceptable while the prime commercial rate hangs around 12.5 percent. State that you can only afford 10 percent, but that you believe he or she will easily gain the difference in goodwill and greater productivity.

Make it clear that this is a confidential request, and that you would keep the arrangement confidential. Do not offer to do any more work—for example, work longer days—unless you deem it to be a reasonable trade-off. And do not get trapped into a tough negotiating session. If you sense that your employer might suddenly seize this opportunity to squeeze you by making excessive demands, you should approach the subject tentatively and as one of a number of possibilities. Say that you feel the need to take out a loan, and since you cannot afford the ridiculous prevailing rates, would it be feasible to discuss other alternatives with him or her at a convenient time? Your tone should be upbeat, hopeful. People who need to borrow often adopt a self-effacing, sad, and even desperate manner. As we have said before, this is a common self-defeating trap. Whom would you rather lend to—a person down on himself or herself, or someone with a "can do" attitude? Keep it in mind when you make your pitch.

Whether you approach friend, family, employer, or credit union, be sure that you stress that you are concerned about creating a favorable credit history for the future. As a part of your repayment plan, state that you would like to be able to write in to a credit bureau relating to your transaction. This should be added stimulus or proof from their point of view that you will take your obligation seriously. No matter how well you know the person that is providing the loan to you, insist that you put the terms into writing to avoid any later misunderstanding and as evidence to the credit bureau, as well as for tax purposes.

Women will continue to have to work harder or get short-changed with regard to their creditworthiness. While women's credit rights have been greatly bolstered in the last eight years, women will remain at a distinct disadvantage until their earning power is commensurate with that of men.

Equity rewards the vigilant—make sure your creditor is not operating under old assumptions that do not apply to you. But remember that credit and its allocation is a judgment call and that there are many methods of subterfuge available to the creditor who simply does not like your attitude. As with most things in life, it is best to avoid the extremes—being brazen is no better than the helpless, hopeless act.

Community Property States

Eight states and the Commonwealth of Puerto Rico have community property laws. Arizona, California, Idaho, Louisiana, Nevada, New Mexico, Texas, and Washington all have state laws where both husband and wife are considered co-owners, with joint control of all property and income acquired during the marriage. Moreover, they are legally responsible for each other's debts and obligations. While married women without jobs generally have a much easier time getting credit in these states, their husbands or another cosigner are almost always required to sign for an extension of credit. In the event of a divorce or separation, the woman's credit history, even if she had a job and income of her own, is apt to be virtually all a matter of joint accounts, a hazy imprint of a woman's personal credit standing at best. There is little either spouse can do to truly separate their creditworthiness, but if the marriage is good, the disadvantages are minimal.

In the event of a breakup, however, there are a few simple steps to follow, especially if the spouse has been delinquent or overindulging in credit. While the creditor has every right to go after both of you for debts incurred by either party while married, keep a separate record of your credit payments and charges, with copies of signed receipts. You will have a better chance of proving later on in a consumer statement to your credit profile that you did not personally draw upon unpaid or delinquent accounts.

The power of credit is a tool that you create by evaluating your past and present lifestyles and presenting those aspects of your life that prove that you are a person who can be trusted. Good credit is an attitude that you bring to infuse new situations as well as to rekindle old alliances. It is your bond; you create it and you care for it.

We have tried to demonstrate how to take charge of your own credit, even in trying circumstances, rather than having it determined for you. In the next chapter, we will show you how to evaluate the pros and cons of various types of credit available to make the most of your credit power.

Chapter Eight

Shopping

for

Credit

ALL CREDIT IS NOT CREATED EQUAL. DIFFERENTIATING BE-tween the costly or imprudent course versus the best path to most profitably ply your credit career is just as important as how you go about establishing your credit in the first place. In the euphoria that often accompanies approval, some people lose perspective regarding the true costs of using a particular credit vehicle. You must keep your wits and take the time to work out whether the deal you are striking is workable over the long term—more than just an indulgent spree or another credit "fix" that will leave you more strung out when it comes due—and whether it is worthwhile from a strictly dollars-and-cents standpoint.

THE CONVENIENCE CANARD

The new age of deregulated services is breaking virtually every day on the front pages of your newspaper's financial section. Analysts speculate about the plausibility of finan-cial supermarkets while banks, insurance companies, and other national and regional businesses forge ahead, acquiring or merging to form new and increasingly odd alliances. Former adversaries unite, incongruous industries meld: an insurance company acquires a stock brokerage, a consumer finance company buys out faltering savings and loan associations, all in the name of diversification.

The big idea behind all of this wheeling and dealing is the notion that convenience will prove to be an irresistible lure to consumers. Not only does diversification allow these larger entities greater economies of scale but, as we have noted, they also provide their customers with more products. Why go further when you can get all of your financial needs handled in one place, from soup to nuts? Why struggle or complicate your life with the confusion of comparing competing services when you can streamline your finances with a well-known, respected, and big company that can offer you a share of its clout? No doubt you will be hearing and reading subtle and not-so-subtle marketing pitches on an increasing basis in the future to the effect that you can only benefit by consolidating your finances, including credit. This is a ruse that can badly diminish and possibly damage your credit potential; do not be conned into consolidating.

Any smart consumer knows that retail companies draw you into their stores with sales on specific merchandise in the hope that, once inside, you will buy other products you need or like that are not on sale. Banks and other financial service companies may be willing to engage in such "loss leaders" in order to gain the rest of your business. Watch out: bear in mind that supposed bargains that preclude that you buy other services may turn out to be more expensive in the long run. Moreover, you have effectively relinquished a large part of your most important asset—your credit. By consolidating for the sake of immediate convenience, you reduce the number of credit references and increase the risk of substantial damage if one or more aspects of that overwrought relationship turns sour.

Shopping for credit rather than succumbing to the con-

venience come-on protects your financial freedom and provides you with an alluring consumer characteristic—you
are versatile. By diversifying your credit, you hold out the
tantalizing possibility that you may one day move some of
your other accounts to any of the companies that you are
already dealing with or to someone completely new.

In the struggle to accumulate larger shares of their markets, diversified financial service companies seem to be
driven during this decade to concentrate on new business
rather than to service current or existing accounts. Let
them play into your hands if you like by adopting a middle
ground of adding or switching an account from another
company, if it makes sense from a cost standpoint, as well
as by considering the loss of ongoing accumulated credit
standing from the discounted creditor. Never put all your
eggs in one basket: to have checking, savings, insurance,
brokerage, mortage closed- and open-end credit based in
one company is idiotic. But you might rightfully benefit by
combining two or more services as long as they do not include brokerage. Later in the chapter we will discuss at
greater length why you should treat any brokerage business
you might consider with special care and under stringent
limitations. For now, let us state the fundamental premise
that commingling various types of financial relationships
under one corporate roof, even if they are separate subsidiaries, is not now and never will be a sage or safe route to
true creditworthiness.

PRICING IN PERSON

The importance of applying in person for any financial
service that involves credit is not only due to its value as a
device to help you get credit, as outlined in previous pages,
but also because it could very well mean a better price. The
posted going rate or fees for certain transactions are not
nonnegotiable; you should ask if certain charges can be
dropped or reduced while your application is still being

processed. Even afterward, you have the right to contest or ask to be excluded from new fees being imposed on certain types of accounts or transactions. This can be done effectively only in person; requests over the phone do not make the grade and letters are only useful as a follow-up to a face-to-face discussion.

Let it be known that you are shopping for the best rates as well as for a personal relationship. It is wise to butter up the banker or other creditors with words that relate your appreciation and respect for said creditor, but you simply cannot afford those rates, and you would be grateful if he or she would help you. Dislodge the "company policy" dodge if necessary by agreeing first, but adding that there is always latitude granted for some good customers, and that you would think they would recognize you as such. If the person claims that he or she doesn't have the authority to waive or discount certain charges or rates, ask who does. Push the "up" button until you feel you are properly accommodated. Many retail businesses use this impotence routine to get rid of nuisance customers. Lower level employees are told to pass the buck up to their superior in certain cases, and then it's up to a secretary to make it as inconvenient as possible to meet. If you find yourself in this position, you have probably either miscalculated the value of your business to the company, not clearly articulated that worth, or are making a truly unreasonable request.

In any event, you should not be shy about asking for a break. It's an accepted business practice to ask for a better deal. It has nothing to do with your credit ability. You are at least entitled to inquire, and many times creditors are empowered to make significant changes in the cost structure of how the business operates. Even if the initial answer is "I'm sorry, no," follow up with a question of how could you qualify or be entitled to the privileges you are seeking, or ask which customers are granted these rights. What you want to ferret out is how you are truly perceived by the creditor. Are you an incidental add-on piece of business to the mainstay clientele of a few or many coporations? Or is it truly a consumer-oriented business, but you're just not considered rich enough? Whatever the rationale, if the creditor advertises for people like yourself to become customers, you should mention that if the firm truly wants to keep your business, it should make a greater effort to accommodate all of its customers.

The study of credit, then, is the measurement of your actual past payments versus your obligations over time. Yet how you are measured, the criteria used to determine character, capacity, and capital commitments, varies widely from company to company. These considerations are based on any number of industry traditions, profit goals, general economic conditions and projections, company strategies to meet them, and other factors, plus your own financial relationship (or lack thereof) with the creditor. These perceptions often conflict: the electric company may consider you a deadbeat while Nieman-Marcus and Merrill Lynch continue to stuff your mailbox with solicitations, courting your cashless patronage. Moreover, company criteria are fluid and apt to change suddenly, especially in the selection of new credit customers. Some credit industry spokesmen privately argue that the Federal Reserve Board has been setting the market in the last decade, requiring more company oversight and eventual cost to the consumer. Given the vagaries of the current economic climate, credit grantors are constantly scrutinizing their market position and readjusting their plans and policies. At any one time, it may prove more difficult to become a new credit card customer at Macy's than to qualify for a Carte Blanche charge card.

In order to establish and maximize your credit potential in America today, you should be aware of these market conditions, as well as of the specific peculiarities of each company with which you deal. Two basic forces are at odds here: mechanized or computerized credit granting versus personal or direct human judgment.

FIGURING FINANCE CHARGES

Whether you are applying for open-end (revolving) or closed-end (installment) loans, you have the right to know, under the Truth-in-Lending Act, what the true finance charges amount to. For installment loans, the creditor must reveal what is the annual percentage rate being charged. It can, however, still quote interest rates in forms other than the annual percentage rate that sound lower than the actual rate of interest paid. Because there are still a lot of unscrupulous lenders who talk a good line and spout figures about "discounted rates" which end up costing you much more, you should insist that you see in writing what the annual percentage rate (APR) is before signing any document.

Even knowing this APR is not enough for open-end lines of credit; you should also be aware of the manner in which the finance charge will be calculated. Since credit card usage is not pegged to a certain dollar figure (other than maximum limit), there isn't any fixed finance charge per se. However, there are three basic methods of computing finance charges that directly affect the cost.

Most credit card issuers calculate their finance charge using the *Average Daily Balance* method. Certain states have laws prohibiting the compounding of finance charges (Maine, Massachusetts) or the graduated application of finance charges on accounts with less than $1,000 due (California). Basically, the method employed involves adding up your balance for each day of the billing period, then dividing by the number of days in the billing period to determine your average balance. Then the creditor multiplies that figure by an equal fraction of the annual percentage rate, based on the total number of billing (called the periodic rate) periods per year. Sounds complicated? It is.

For example, let's take an instance where a department store's finance charge is 18 percent per year. On a $100 credit purchase, you pay $10 in the middle of the first billing cycle. To make it easy, let's assume there are monthly billing cycles. The periodic rate is 1.5 percent (18% ÷ 12). Since, for the first half of the month, your balance was $100, and the second half it was $90, the average daily balance during the month comes to $95. Multiply: $95 × 1.5% = $1.43. Assuming you make no additional purchases during the month, your next bill will state $91.43 due.

A few credit grantors still get away with calculating finance charges using the *Previous Balance* method (Nieman-Marcus, for one). Under this system, there are no credits given for payments during the billing period and the finance charge is levied on the entire amount owed at the beginning of the month. So, even though you paid $10 on the $100 credit purchase, your finance charge for the month is $100 × 1.5% = $1.50. Seven cents difference between average daily balance and previous balance methods may seem like small change, but these costs are compounded year in and year out by the faithful charge customer.

The third and hardly used method of calculating finance charges is the *Adjusted Balance* method, where the monthly finance charge is computed after directly subtracting payments made during the billing period. On the same $100 credit purchase with $10 payment during the first billing period, the finance charge would come to $90 × 1.5% = $1.35. You can see why adjusted balance has fallen out of favor except where required by law.

SOURCES OF CREDIT
The following sources of credit are all legitimate for certain circumstances. You need not involve yourself with all or even most of these creditors, but they are viable options, given the proper conditions. The procedures, benefits, and pitfalls are discussed individually.

Commercial Banks
The old tried-and-true method of establishing credit is to open a savings account at a bank (usually along with a

checking account), wait a few months, and then ask for a short-term loan for an amount equivalent to what you had in your savings account. Passbook loans, they're called. Today, however, too many banks impose a minimum loan level way beyond the grasp of most people seeking an initial experience with credit. Swallow this: Many banks surveyed claim they cannot make any money on loans less than $2,500. At current consumer interest charges exceeding 15 percent, as of this writing, that's $375 in simple interest for a one-year loan on this amount. Bankers contest, in turn, that they loan money on funds borrowed at only one or two percentage points below their loan rate, for a real gross margin of $25 to $50, which is not enough to cover their overhead. Nonsense. When the calculator replaces the mind and heart of banking, this myopic form of number-gazing becomes the dull weapon to befuddle the small banking customer right out of the system. In fact, a loan one half this size—or even $1,000—must be considered potentially profitable, especially when the customer already has or agrees to establish savings and checking accounts. Any amount you bring into the bank in these accounts is cheap money for the bank and must be considered in an evaluation of its profit margin.

For example, if you have an average of $500 in your savings and checking accounts earning 5 percent interest or $25 a year, you are granting the bank the right to loan out $2,500, or five times its asset base, under Federal Reserve Board regulations. And, remember, banks typically try to charge at least two points above the prime commercial lending rate for unsecured consumer loans. Bank of America recently has been charging its consumers for unsecured loans between 5½ to *12 percent* above the prime commercial rate. Hence any money in savings or checking accounts is virtually found money today, with banks making anywhere from 10 to 17 percent gross profit five times over the amount in the accounts.

The more fundamental benefit to the bank—one which

defies precise calculative formulations—is the value of a satisfied customer, a truly grateful customer who represents repeat and long-term business if the banker is simply decent and fosters a sympathetic bond. If commercial banks really want their consumer business to survive this decade intact, they must work harder at humanizing their heretofore feeble attempts at providing people with personal, professional service at prices less than usurious. The physical existence of consumer banking is currently being actively threatened by finely marketed near-bank competitors. As the central force of the credit system, commercial banks must recognize that their principal edge is their established and highly visible branch personnel system, which could allow for more local autonomy to accommodate and care for their customers. If banks continue the present trend of reneging on their traditional leadership role in helping people establish credit at a reasonable entry level, the vacuum will be filled by savvy savings and loans, credit unions, and other newer financial service companies.

Keep this in mind when you consider various sources from which to build your credit. Their moral imperative to help you is a powerful position for you to address. Creditors that appear impervious to this rationale, that insist that their overriding concern is meeting their margins, are not to be trusted. The heart-of-stone stereotype lives, but why should you continue to feed it once you recognize it? Remember, trust is a two-way street: your savings represent lending money to the bank at low rates. Why should you pay two to four times that rate when you want money loaned back? The commercial banks most culpable in this regard are the international giants who have diversified their holdings to such an extent that they no longer have a real stake in the community. They are consistently the most flagrant violators of the Community Reinvestment Act, a law that tries to make banks put some of the money they take out of an area back in. These banks typically charge more for everything, from loans to penalty charges for dipping below minimum balances to stop payment orders on checks. Every type of transaction is a "profit center" to these brigand bankers. You can actually lose money today putting it in one of these banks unless you come up with $500, $1,000, or even more.

What makes this trend all the more insidious is the fact that these multinational banks have the gall and the bucks to throw around to try to cuddle up to the consumer. Huge sums have been anted up for advertising budgets that extoll their alleged manifold virtues of convenience, expertise, and clout. Citibank, Chase Manhattan, Bank of America, Security Pacific, Continental Illinois, Manufacturers Hanover, Chemical of New York, and scores of other banks have sunk millions of dollars into expanding their consumer divisions. Citibank was the first to spend outrageous sums (reportedly $500 million) on computerizing its entire worldwide network to gear up for grabbing a large chunk of the national consumer market. The trouble is that its current customers are paying dearly for what amounts to defraying these research and development costs.

It remains to be seen whether these giant commercial banks will be able to pull off what amounts to one of the largest consumer coups of the century. They are counting on a major "consolidation" of existing commercial banks as well as the ability to control or kill off all but a small percentage of savings and loan associations. To date, the nonsensically high interest rates seem to be playing right into their hands. The problem that lies ahead in the not-so-distant future is that there will remain always a very basic difference between commercial and consumer banking— one is wholesale and the other is a retail business. Their thinking is that electronic banking will allow them to increase their consumer funds' asset base while limiting personnel growth to approach commercial or wholesale levels. In other words, kiss your personal banker goodbye, or at least be prepared to stand on an awfully long line in the future.

In the meantime, there is still hope for the smaller commercial banks in good markets that do not get seduced by all those costly bells and whistles of electronic banking. People like to do business with folks they know and who know them beyond an account number. Large interstate and intercontinental banks may be initially successful in landing a large number of impressionable new accounts, but people will eventually alter their impressions when they realize that machines and all the coming wonders of electronic funds transfer are no match for personal interaction in building your credit. Beyond the certainty of multifarious electronic nightmares involving the mysterious disappearance of your money, the dangers of electronic banking include the potential for abrupt and volatile swings of your credit, or the loss of it entirely, depending on the wizardry of a handful of technicians tinkering continually out of sight. Approach electronic banking with extreme caution, if at all. It is convenience gone berserk. And now the French, who still can't get their phone system to work, are planning to leapfrog into an elaborate national home computer communication and financial transfer system. So-called smart cards with embedded microchips will allow consumers to walk around with "loaded" plastic that gets deducted upon inserting it into another machine when making purchases. Let's let them work the bugs out of that first before adopting it on our shores. Beyond 1984, please.

Once you find a suitable bank with a banker who actually metabolizes, an alternate way to establish your creditworthiness is to go ahead and request a $2,500 loan and stipulate that the loan money will be placed in a savings account to be held by the bank. This should qualify you for the prime commercial rate. After all, you are paying the bank in two ways: the interest on the loan, and the ability to reloan the same money five times over. Resist paying more than prime.

A variation on this method is to formalize this relationship by collateralizing the loan with the new savings account. Freeze it, except for use in paying back the loan. Try to avoid this less-than-optimal arrangement. Any collateralized loan is a relatively weak demonstration of credit-worthiness because credit is trust, and that hasn't been proven in a fully collateralized loan. A banker will reap the same profit with the money in the unsecured savings account.

A six-month loan, or prepaying after the first six months, may be a less costly method to establish credit if there are no substantial prepayment penalties. Negotiate. What you want is the least costly method of demonstrating your ability and willingness to repay while satisfying the banker's threshold of comfort. Maybe a life insurance policy covering the term of your loan would clinch the deal. Or a safe-deposit box if that makes sense for you.

Finding a co-obligor for your loan is another popular way to break the credit barrier with a commercial bank or any other financial institution. In the event you cannot make your payments, your parents, relative, or friend—whoever signed—must pay off your debt or continue payments until you can assume them again. Getting someone to agree to be your co-obligor can be a casual or formal business deal. Perhaps the only inducement necessary is a promise to take the person out on the town when you successfully pay off the loan. A more formal route could entail writing up a separate side contract that pays the individual a stipulated amount—like an FHA guaranty mortgage insurance contract.

Once you have paid off a co-obligor loan on schedule, you have demonstrated good credit and will have a much better chance of getting your next loan on your signature alone, all other things being equal.

Savings and Loan Associations
Savings and loan associations were founded to make mortgage loans for middle America. Their current plight is due to carrying many low-priced mortgages at rates way

below their current cost of acquiring money. Many S & Ls have mortgages out at 6, 7, and 8 percent while it costs them more than 10 percent on average for the money loaned still on the books. The outflow of funds from their savings accounts into other higher interest bearing accounts has further aggravated their current financial strain. Clearly, these are not rosy times for the thrifts.

So why bother even considering doing business with the down-and-seemingly-almost-out savings and loan crowd? Opportunity, in a word. First, your money is safe—it is federally insured, as you know, up to $100,000 per account. In all the mergers and bailouts to date, no depositors have lost one cent. Stockholders are another matter—you can get burned there. Second, deregulation moves now allow savings and loans to offer money-market instruments bearing as high an interest as practically anywhere else (although uninsured, as is the case elsewhere).

Precisely because the thrifts are in a pinch right now, your present loyalty should be worth future credit. Make an appointment with an officer of the bank and let it be known (unpretentiously) that you want to help them but want to make sure that your goodwill will be remembered when *you* need a helping hand. Savings and loans in most states are now allowed to make all sorts of consumer loans. Many, however, are publicly out of the loan market entirely, except for the occasional mortgage that dribbles in. This will not do. Now that most S & Ls are allowed, there is no excuse for not exercising the second half of their titles. Consumer loans at prime for loyal customers would make good news for once. They can handle them despite excuses that they are not properly equipped. All they do these days is pretend they are investment bankers by moving money around in overnight funds.

Beware of the new, large interstate savings and loans as a rule unless you already have a personal relationship with someone in management. Friendly tellers don't count.

Credit Unions

One of your best bets in establishing credit may be to join one of the more than 21,000 credit unions operating throughout the country today. More than 45 million Americans are currently members. A credit union is a cooperative organization owned and controlled by its members for the purpose of saving money and making this money available to one another for loans.

Qualifying for membership in a credit union is based upon fulfilling a "common bond" requirement—people who work for the same company, church, club, or union; or people who simply live in the same community. All credit unions are limited by geographic area; there are no interstate credit unions.

The most obvious benefits of belonging to a credit union are that they generally charge their members lower rates for loans and grant higher rates for regular savings than other financial institutions. Because they are not-for-profit organizations whose officers and directors serve without pay, except for the treasurer, the members are rewarded with any excess earned in dividends, and rebates on loans. But the benefits go a lot deeper than competitive rates, as alluring as these can be.

Credit unions are chartered to give a group of similar people the ability to help each other increase their credit potential. There is much less overhead and no outside stockholders demanding increased profits. The members are the stockholders, and they elect their officers and directors from their own ranks. Each member gets one vote, regardless of the number of shares held, or the amount he or she has invested in the credit union.

But how safe is your money? All federally chartered credit unions are required to be insured up to $100,000 per member by the National Credit Union Administration's Share Insurance Fund (which is the equivalent of the Federal Reserve Board's Federal Deposit Insurance Corporation). Most state-chartered credit unions are also insured by the same agency or by a comparable state agency. Yet six states (Idaho, Indiana, Nebraska, New Hampshire, New Jersey, and Oklahoma) do not require insurance. Before joining a credit union, make sure that it is insured; 97 percent are insured.

It's also a good idea to investigate the reputation of the credit union before you join. There are admittedly some that leave something to be desired with regard to the quality of their service, due to inadequate staffing or simply because of colleagues who are not qualified to do the job. Always check with someone you know who is a member.

The deregulation that is spreading throughout the financial services industry arrived first for the credit unions. They are allowed to engage in virtually every type of transaction allowed to commercial banks except leveraging their money. Considering that any credit union's membership is often drawn from people in the same profession or company, it seems wise to preclude a credit union from extending credit beyond its asset base, thereby fully covering its loan exposure at all times.

Obviously, small church or community development credit unions that are oriented toward people in depressed neighborhoods cannot and often do not even wish to offer the wide range of services available to larger, better heeled credit unions typically associated with one large employer or industry. The larger credit unions are more likely to hire their own paid managers rather than to rely solely on paid treasurer and his or her cadre of volunteers. Still, a great deal of professional support is routinely extended to all from the very smallest of credit unions through state credit union leagues and their corporate arm. Leagues are voluntary organizations comprised of credit unions that give operating advice and assistance, education and training, legal assistance, research and governmental relations services to their member credit unions. Leagues also help form new credit unions. More than 90 percent of all credit unions are members of their state credit union leagues. In 42 states, separate league-owned services corporations called corporate credit unions provide credit unions with necessary business and financial products to help them operate more effectively. Clearly, a solid support system exists for state and federally chartered credit unions to continue to function and even flourish in the future.

All credit unions offer savings plans and make loans to their members. Many, if not most, now offer interest-earning checking accounts (called share drafts) and provide additional savings plans including certificate accounts, Individual Retirement Accounts, and All-Savers. Most also offer free insurance programs such as life savings and credit life, and many provide as well travelers' checks, money orders, and check cashing at no charge. Federally chartered credit unions may also:

• make loans to members for any purpose for up to 12 years on a secured or unsecured basis
• finance home mortgages for members up to 30 years
• finance home improvement loans for up to 15 years
• offer credit cards (VISA or MasterCard) or other types of line-of-credit loans
• provide any government insured or guaranteed loans, state or federal, on terms, conditions, and maturities specified in the loan program

While state-chartered credit unions may vary somewhat from state to state, their specific powers are mostly similar to those of federal credit unions. The types of services offered largely reflect the desires of their members. For instance, many credit unions had to make the choice between offering its members higher yielding savings plans or keeping its very low-cost loans. In order to keep their asset base up, many credit unions now have a large percentage of their savings accounts in money-market type funds, and their loan rates have risen accordingly.

Still, many larger credit unions are able to provide great additional benefits: cars to members at just above the manufacturer's price, and discounts on a wide array of other merchandise and services, including car rentals. Many also provide free financial counseling and conduct continuing education programs on money and budgeting.

As a source of credit, credit unions often write into their charters extremely accommodating notions about the loan process. Quite a number of them stipulate that the loan committee must be unanimous in rejecting an application before a final decision can be reached. Moreover, we discovered time after time a refreshingly open and caring approach to people evident among credit union officials. The personal touch that banks are paying lipservice to, credit unions are actually giving.

How do you join? It may take a bit of doing. Credit unions are not open to the general public so you have to find one locally where you can comply with their common bond constriction. Almost all credit unions extend membership to the immediate family, so if someone in your family can join one, that usually entitles you to join. And most credit unions state in their charters that "once a member, always a member," so it would be wise to join up while the opportunity is there. Some large employer-based credit unions have become community credit unions, allowing members within a certain proximity to the plant to join whether they work for it or not. And a number of teachers' credit unions define their common bond to extend to anyone who has a child in the local public school system. Look in the Yellow Pages under "Credit Unions" and check Appendix D for your state credit union league.

The diversity of credit unions is astounding. There are credit unions for certain ethnic groups, again always on a local basis: Ukrainians, Spanish, Chinese, and Polish, to name just a few. And in different localities, there are credit unions for almost every religious persuasion. California has at least one gay credit union, and there is a feminist credit union based in Boston.

If you cannot find a credit union for your needs after consulting with your state league, and feel that you can muster up a legitimate group of at least 200 people united in some fashion who live within a close proximity, consider starting your own credit union. It takes a tremendous amount of work and you need a core group of dedicated volunteers, but you can usually count on technical and psychological support from state credit union officials to guide you along.

For those who have or create their own common bond, credit unions can be the actualization of taking control of their own credit destiny. They will gladly comply with most requests to help improve your credit, including the reporting of any transaction to credit bureaus.

Bank Credit Cards (VISA, MasterCard)

Both VISA and MasterCard license their plastic cards to subscribing banks and other financial institutions. Once upon a time just a few years ago, there was no annual fee for these cards, but more and more banks are charging between $15 and $25 annually for either basic card and up to $40–$50 for the gold or international versions. Shop around for a bank that still offers these cards at no charge, but be sure to check that there are no other, perhaps more costly, "strings" attached to these supposedly "free" cards.

When you apply for one of these cards you are really applying for a bank loan—it's a commitment to lend to you when you wish. As such, you should follow the same strategies outlined in earlier chapters. The spending limit the banks sets amounts to your level of creditworthiness, but you should also view it as a reasonable figure considering a prudent course of buying and as a stopgap source of emergency credit. In other words, don't let your ego inflate your credit limit here; rates are typically way above prime, so it is not a good source for long- and large-term credit.

Criteria for acceptance vary according to the bank's past experience with other cardholders. Today, there is often a $15,000 to $20,000 minimum annual income level to be considered eligible for either VISA or MasterCard. The best way to challenge or seek an exemption from the bank's normal income or ratio requirements is through the personal interview. Despite the bank's inclination to keep bank card relationships confined to the mail, you should insist that you meet with a lending officer to discuss the merits of your case.

My father, at age 75, was initially denied a VISA card because he was retired. He and my mother spent two and a half hours with a banker and explained that, although they were retired, he was building a new source of income. He had become an artist, had recently been exhibited locally, and was beginning to sell his work. Worn down or whatever, the banker finally relented and approved his new application; today, my father is considered a good VISA customer of the bank. Again, my father offers proof that you can overcome the normal dynamics involved in the granting of credit by *personal perseverance*.

The tremendous demand for MasterCard and VISA cards by people who have been rejected for such service has resulted in the proliferation of a relatively new kind of credit opportunist—the credit "middleman" who locates a bank that is willing to issue cards to anyone, provided that the usage is limited or secured to the amount in a savings account. For a hefty "professional fee"—as much as $100 or even more—that they keep, and between $250 and $600 to be put in a savings account in some (usually obscure) bank, you are given a card, regardless of your income or credit standing.

The Better Business Bureau and the U.S. Postal Service, among other authorities, are cracking down on these flim-flam operations, which often disappear after they receive your money. Some are legitimate, however, including Timesaver Inc. and the United Savings and Loan Association of Vienna, Virginia. They do make credit checks, although they are running into problems with all sorts of unscrupulous outfits falsely claiming to be authorized agents of Timesaver Inc.

If you are tempted to apply for one of these credit cards because you have been rejected or fear that your past credit experience will cause a denial, consider this option instead. Make an appointment with a loan officer of the bank you are now dealing with and tell him or her that you want to improve your credit rating and are willing to secure your VISA or MasterCard to an amount you have kept on balance. Even if you currently have no income, a banker should not object to "freezing" or collateralizing your savings account. Make sure you get the banker to initial the application so that a clerk does not proceed mechanically. Your objective should be to work within this type of arrangement for six months or a year (during which time be certain you pay immediately upon receipt of the bill) until such time as your credit rating may become strong enough to assure your banker and other creditors that you are now worthy of their (unsecured) credit.

Charge Cards

A charge card should not be confused with a credit card. Charge cards operate on a pay-as-you-go basis (per billing cycle) while a credit card allows you to postpone complete payment as long as you continue to pay the interest charges and at least part of the principal. American Express, Diners Club, and Carte Blanche are all charge cards. (Both Diners and Carte Blanche were bought out by Citicorp, the parent company of Citibank.)

Charge cards charge an annual fee—between $35 and $50 currently—for their various financial services, which can include personal loans for some of their customers. Normally, though, because payment of the total bill is due upon receipt, charge cards should inhibit the temptation to spend more money than you can realistically afford. These cards are properly used as travel and expense tools for business and vacation purposes, but they are also honored at an increasing number of department stores and specialty shops.

Charge cards are valuable sources of emergency credit

and are most helpful credit references for getting other credit cards and privileges. Use one or more of these cards wisely; while not all of them report your record of payment to the credit bureaus, you can take the initiative to insert a good history into your credit profile (as shown in Chapter 2).

Retail Credit Cards

Retail credit cards are among the least expensive and simplest ways to establish and/or improve your financial history. These include department store, gas, airline, and car rental cards. There is usually no initial or annual charge for these cards, and they often grant you as much as 30 days on your purchases before imposing interest charges. Some airline and other credit cards occasionally offer as much as 3 to 10 months to pay off a bill without interest charges to spur sales. After the first billing period expires, interest charges are typically the maximum allowed under state law, so it is both costly and stupid to allow these payments to lag.

Retail credit cards are marketing tools for the companies that make them available to their customers. These companies want to help make it as easy as possible for you to buy more, including phone orders. As such, the criteria they establish for acceptance are often based on who they perceive are their most desirable potential customers. Adequate income is what they look for most: many department stores require their new cardholders to have minimum incomes ranging from $15,000 to more than $30,000, though few will admit to it publicly, for fear of alienating cash customers.

We heard from one woman who, after becoming exasperated by the succession of department stores that insisted on their need to know her income, finally wrote in $100,000 as her income on one application just for a laugh. That particular store card arrived in the mail within days while the cards for the other department stores—where she either left the income question blank or wrote in her true income of $12,000 on the application—never arrived. While retail credit card companies may often verify employment over the phone (some don't even bother doing that), corroborating income is often too delicate or difficult a matter to accomplish efficiently.

While applying for retail credit cards is a relatively simple way to improve and add to your credit, many times you must already possess an established and positive credit history on file with the local credit bureau. Again, the old credit "Catch-22." Especially during times of contraction in the local economy, many creditors become tougher about assessing your signs of stability and good credit. When people are being laid off, factories are closing up, and businesses are sitting on inventories that won't move, creditors are not looking to grant more credit—they want cash. In this environment, people without an established credit profile or who have a new-in-town status with less than superlative past credentials need not bother to apply by mail.

For department stores, at least, you should go down in person to the credit department of the store if there is any question about whether you will qualify for a card. And don't go during business hours if you claim you have a job on the application. Most are open late and on weekends for the convenience of their customers.

Sears Roebuck cards traditionally have been relatively easy to get if you have a job, as are many gas and car rental cards (provided you own a car) and some airline credit cards. But be sure you are in fact going to benefit from the use of these cards. Just because you are granted credit with certain companies does not mean you should use their services. One fellow from Houston we came across used to operate in an opposite fashion. After he got out of college, he began calling up all the stores and other businesses he could think of to ask for credit applications; he got them, filled them out, and waited. Whoever sent him cards back was subject to a shopping spree. "It was like a license to steal. I didn't know how I was going to pay back, but my attitude was, well, they sent me the card, so it's okay to use it." Today, this hit-or-miss approach will seldom work because just about every credit grantor checks or makes an inquiry with a local credit bureau. Once a credit grantor sees another or a number of other recent inquiries on the credit bureau report, the grantor gets suspicious quickly and joins the club that denies credit. For up to three to seven years later, this batch of inquiry lines on a bureau report can inhibit another credit grantor from approving your credit request.

Still, all kinds of strange and crazy credit stories pop up. A New Jersey woman recently related with wonder how she was accepted for her Bloomingdale's card by filling out an in-store salesperson's application within days after being rejected for the same store card applied for through the mail. One application obviously had been checked and stopped by the store's credit department while the other was later approved by Bloomingdale's marketing department.

Another woman from Dallas was understandably furious when her request for a credit card from Sakowitz was denied. She called up and demanded an explanation. They said that there was not enough information about her on record with the local credit bureau. She countered that she had a good job for three years, an American Express account, and Lord & Taylor and Nieman-Marcus credit cards, all of which she acknowledged on her application. The credit office wanted her to come down to their office to identify herself and show them. Instead of complying, she wrote an angry letter to the president with a carbon to the credit department that stated: (1) she had been solicited through the mail to apply for the card; (2) she decided to fill out the application because she shopped at the store and liked its catalogue; (3) she supplied a number of credit references that undeniably demonstrated her creditworthiness; and (4) because they were too lazy to pick up the phone to verify this information, she didn't want a credit card from Sakowitz and, moreover, she would never shop there again. Three days later a credit card came from the credit office, and the following day another Sakowitz card arrived from the president's office. She still has not used the card or shopped at the store.

Most oil company credit cards, while relatively easy to obtain, do not bother to report to a credit bureau. Amoco, with its 7 million credit card customers, naturally wants to avoid the expense of reporting the transactions of all these people to credit bureaus all over the country. So do most of the other major oil companies with credit cards. Consequently, their value as a credit reference is normally nil. And in the past, everyone had gas charge cards and the bills did not add to much.

With today's inflated prices, you can effectively authorize the release of a potentially significant positive credit reference by writing for your repayment record with the total amount billed yearly. By consolidating gas purchases to one card for a period of time, you can clearly demonstrate creditworthiness with significant sums of money.

Not all retail credit grantors are sanguine about the business. Arco decided to drop its 3 million card customers in order to save its dealers the 3 percent carrying cost of accepting credit. And in different portions of the country other retailers have abandoned credit card purchases, especially discount merchandisers like Woolworth, Times Square Stores, and Channel.

Other credit granting companies suspend credit card privileges or let them expire without reissuing new ones if the card is not used frequently enough. Therefore, upon acceptance, find out if the credit grantor stipulates certain minimum levels of activity. A suspension of card privileges, which could find its way onto your credit profile, generally looks worse than not having the card in the first place.

Before using your retail credit card, find out: (1) the day of the month the billing period ends, and (2) exactly how many days after the billing date your payment has to be postmarked in order for your account to be cleared as current. Many companies lop off as many as five days and work on a 25-day rather than a 30-day current account cycle. By the time you receive the bill in the mail and take into account the time needed to send it back through the mail, you often have less than a week to keep the interest charges from mounting. Savvy consumers are very aware of exactly when a billing cycle ends and take advantage of a few more days of float by charging on the day after the billing cycle closes.

Investment Companies

It is becoming increasingly difficult to distinguish between investment companies, banks, and consumer finance companies. With Sears Roebuck and Prudential anteing up billions to diversify their financial services, and dozens of others quickly following suit by acquiring brokerages, savings and loans, consumer finance companies, and mortgage companies, it's hard to keep track of who is in what business.

As with the banks, it's called the consolidation game, with giants like Sears Roebuck swiftly transforming itself through acquisitions. "Our goal is to become the largest consumer-oriented financial service entity," states Edward L. Telling, current chairman of the board. A large part of Sears Roebuck's strategy is to convert many of the 40 million credit card accounts to its other products.

Unfettered by banking regulations that still prohibit interstate deposits, a rash of brokerage firms have established big budget mutual funds that offer checking privileges, high interest, and certain aspects of credit. Merrill Lynch, for example, requires a $20,000 minimum for its Cash Management Account, thereby granting you a VISA card good for up to a $5,000 cash advance, free checks, and money-market rates on your portfolio fund if you choose.

While these may be fantastic investment vehicles—the money-market funds have attracted over $200 billion to date—their pseudobanking frills of bank cards and checking should not be confused with an alternate means of building your credit. Any purchase you make with your credit card or with checks is immediately withdrawn from your account. That's not credit—that's just transferring or withdrawing money from your account. A CMA check does, however, tell everyone that you have at least $20,000 in cash and/or securities.

Buying securities on margin is a truer form of credit, being extended to the customers of brokers in degrees. These are loans that many brokers pass on to their customers at "broker loan rates," typically at or slightly below the prime commercial rate. Brokers will only make these loans in order to close a transaction that entitles them to a commission. Brokers make this extension of credit seem like a big deal. Don't be so impressed: your local bookie also operates in the same way. If you lose the bet or if the price of your stock, bond, or commodity option plummets, you better be prepared to come up with the cash quickly.

There are a host of details to be aware of and watch out for concerning dealing with securities brokers—over price and their degree of autonomy in making changes in your portfolio, including credit (too many to adequately address here). However, a word of caution when considering a relationship with any investment company: Aside from individuals who use discount brokerages merely to execute their own investment decisions (which requires both expertise and confidence), it is best not to commingle savings with investment funds in the same company, however separate the various subsidiaries appear to be. In the securities business, integrity and expertise are paramount. Yet among companies like Prudential, which bought Bache, the allure to expand their customer base will inevitably lead to situations where it will be tempting to compromise. A broker is a salesperson usually paid or granted raises on the basis of the volume of his commissions. Naturally, he or she wants an ever increasing pool of funds on which to trade. If your savings are in a safe instrument like government-secured bonds processed by the investment company, or life insurance policies that have savings or investment features, one day your broker is going to want to take advantage of a "unique opportunity" or "special situation" and move that money elsewhere. If the broker can see it, the money is too close.

Personal or Consumer Finance Companies

The traditional personal or consumer finance company is passé for all but the desperate or ignorant. As lousy as banks and other credit grantors are and will become in service and price, most personal finance companies will continue to be worse—that is, the ones that survive. For while the grip that personal finance companies find themselves in is different than what ails the thrifts, the squeeze is just as debilitating. They are stuck in a rut between a high cost to buy or borrow money on the open commercial market and certain regulatory ceilings on consumer rates that many states still stick by. In addition, they are being bounced off the floor by profligate bankrupts, and by a selectively devastating economy.

What to do? Run for shelter, like your house. The big national and regional consumer finance companies like Beneficial and Household are trying to clean up their image and kiss off the great unwashed. No more high-priced, unsecured loans for low-income stiffs. Now these sharpies want high-priced loans secured by your house. Of course, there will always be the friendly inner-city local personal finance company to "service" or stick up the unsophisticated minorities.

But the biggest laugh is the developing strategy of many of the megabanks. They have been forming their own, or gobbling up just about all of the biggest, independent consumer finance companies at bargain basement prices. BankAmerica owns FinanceAmerica, Citicorp bought Person-to-Person, Security Pacific formed Security Pacific Finance out of an amalgam of regionals, and so it goes. These banks seem to be big believers in, not a brave new world of financial services, but a cocky new world where their way goes. It looks like this: You may bank, or rather place your deposits and use checks from these banks, but if you want a loan, please go to the consumer finance division (unless you're talking big bucks). Loan rates for consumers will remain high—significantly higher than commercial rates—despite no appreciable difference in the cost of servicing. Consumers will be seduced by oodles of money spent on friendly marketing, and the press will not squawk much because it is being fed fat advertising contracts.

Don't count on this scenario. Notwithstanding the 10 to 20 percent of Americans who believe anything and everything they see on television, you cannot fool many of the people for any significant length of time. Word gets around: go local for a better deal. Generally avoid personal finance companies—there should always be a better way.

Commercial Credit Companies

Here we are drawing a distinction between general consumer finance companies and those owned or operating for the primary benefit of a select or captive market. They are usually subsidiaries of large manufacturers of durable consumer goods: cars, boats, washing machines, and so on.

While traditionally you could count on getting a better deal on an auto loan from a bank, the current high-interest, low-sales environment that carmakers find themselves in today has induced them to offer low-priced financing as a marketing tool to stimulate sales. If you don't have cash for a new car (which should entitle you to a significant break off the sticker price), be sure to consider the finance or acceptance corporations of the big three automakers.

Several yacht manufacturers are following suit with discount financing programs of their own. Most require a 20 percent to 25 percent down payment and allow for a payback period stretching out as long as 15 years. Their interest rate subsidies have been ranging from 2 percent to 5 percent off the "normal" commercial bank loan rate, depending upon the cost of the vessel, so it definitely pays for you to shop around for the best financing.

In general, seller financing has become a more competitive source of credit for consumer durables. Consider it when talking over price with any dealer. Often, dealers will relent or give back a portion or all of their piece of the financing in order to close the sale.

Family/Friends/Employer

Most people look upon relatives and friends as a last-resort source for credit after exhausting all other avenues. Putting the touch on someone is a distasteful and often embarrassing scene where both parties feel unnecessarily uncomfortable.

It's all in the attitude. First, you should consider approaching these nonprofessional credit sources in exactly the same fashion that you would deal with a bank. Prepare beforehand so that you are certain how much money you need over what length of time and how you will pay it back. Second, be realistic in the interest charge you should pay this person: most people with a fair amount of extra cash have it parked in a money-market mutual fund. You should be prepared to pay at least that amount, if not the commercial bank prime rate. A close family member or friend may initially refuse to accept any interest payment at all—"After all, what are friends for?" Do not allow this person to let you take advantage of him or her in this manner. While the person may protest and even act angry or hurt at your insistence on proceeding in a businesslike fashion, your response should be that you value your relationship too much to have it unfairly tested. This person is doing you a favor by granting you the loan. The least you can do is make sure he or she is not losing money from lack of interest on the deal. Where would the money be coming from? If it's out-of-pocket cash that would normally find its way into a savings account paying 5 percent to 5½ percent, cover that and then some, at the very least.

Your rationale for going to friends or family or even your

employer if you have a relationship that approaches a solid level of trust is simply that you would rather give the interest to them than to a bank.

Avoid installment loans except for instances when you're asking for a lot of money over a long term. It's just a headache to deal with amortization and, if you can plan your financial matters properly, it should be easier for you also to pay the person back with one lump sum at an agreed-upon, predetermined date. A friend of mine hit me up for $50 and wanted to pay me back $5 a week for 11 weeks, or some such deal. I told him, "Don't make my life more difficult. Take your time, but pay me back with one payment, and you owe me one cab fare."

For loans over a couple hundred dollars, put the loan agreement in writing for two reasons. First, it is necessary so there are no misunderstandings later. Second (and this is what you should stress), you want proof for your financial records—interest payments are tax-deductible—and this is also a golden opportunity to add positive credit data to your credit bureau report. This should further ensure that your friend will have confidence in your willingness to repay.

Neighborhood Storeowner
The neighborhood drugstore or hardware store or bar is a good place to cultivate for emergency credit or cashing checks after banking hours. Many shopowners readily accept this responsibility as part of being a good neighbor to regular customers. If you are currently unable to get a charge or credit card, getting to know the proprietor of a neighborhood restaurant or other establishment's open nights could be at least a partial solution to your need for emergency credit.

REAL ESTATE CREDIT
The importance of real estate to consumers requires a separate discussion of the distinct credit procedures and problem areas to negotiate.

As a real estate lawyer, banker, and active real estate purchaser, I have sat on either side of the desk at numerous closings. We cannot adequately deal with all the intricacies involved in the many types of mortgage transactions here. A real estate lawyer should be consulted for any purchase. But before we talk about the various categories of mortgages being made at present, keep this in mind: the terms of a mortgage should be seen as involving one of the most significant uses of your credit. For such an important purchase, naturally emotions play a part. Yet nearly everyone cannot afford to let emotions run wild. Real estate is not an "impulse purchase." I've seen frequent scenes where people "fall in love" with a piece of property and agree immediately to any asking price and terms. One couple I know, for example, fell in love with a house overlooking the Hudson River. The broker took them down a rustic cattle path to the splendid property. He was very quiet. He let them drink in the view, and they said, "It's ours." Later, when the couple's lawyer asked for a survey of the property, they discovered that there was no road to the property. It was landlocked; there was no access, no right of way. The only approach was by helicopter or by boat—with a 1,000-foot ladder.

Because a large measure of your continuing creditworthiness is going to be tied to your mortgage terms, make sure you review them in light of additional credit obligations as a total manageable load. If you sense that it's a tough proposition as is, go back and ask for a better deal. Bargain. Use your good credit record to date as an asset that will relieve the creditor of the worry of late payments. Frame the discussion in terms of satisfying mutual needs or desires for trust. For more than any other type of credit, the long-term mortgage should be viewed as a marriage of sorts.

REAL ESTATE LOANS

It's still Apple Pie in America to borrow in order to buy a home, but simple days of 20- to 30-year mortgages at relatively low, fixed interest rates have disppeared. Double digit rates and stiff competition for funds have forced savings as well as commercial banks to develop new types of mortgages with flexible interest rates and terms. The risk of rising interest rates has been shifted from lenders to consumers, so you have to shop carefully to protect yourself while finding a mortgage that suits your needs.

When institutional lenders review your application, they look for three things: (1) positive credit history; (2) your ability to make the monthly payments; and (3) satisfactory "loan-to-value" relationship of the property (also called the debt-to-equity ratio—that is, the mortgage debt divided by the market value of the property).

The same rules for evaluating your creditworthiness apply to real estate loans. Your ability to pay back is usually gauged against a traditional industry formula: the total monthly payment of interest, amortization, real estate insurance, and taxes should not exceed 35 percent of your disposable income each month. Citibank sets the figure at 30 percent maximum; each bank tends to develop its own particular rationale for what amounts to mortgage scoring. But you can quarrel with these formulas simply by showing your own budget, which reflects the peculiarities of *you*, not some abstract formula. While the loan-to-value relationship is an aspect that each lender considers differently, in general, all only want to lend you a portion of the market value of a property, so that they are assured of getting their money back in the event of a foreclosure and the ensuing action (which always yields less than market value). An 80 percent loan ratio, for example, might be one in which you obtained an $80,000 mortgage for a home with an appraised value of $100,000.

Of course, it's important that you demonstrate to a mortgagee your creditworthiness and the investment potential of your property, but it's even more important for the lender to demonstrate to *you* that his or her mortgage has the right stuff. A good mortgage can be a real asset, giving your property enhanced value for potential resale in to-

day's scrambled marketplace. A bad mortgage, on the other hand—say, an "uncapped" adjustable-rate mortgage in
which sharp increases in interest rates are suddenly passed
on to you—might wreak havoc with your monthly budget
or might place you in a position of owing more than the
property is worth, putting you in a tough spot should you
need to sell.

If you approach an institutional lender (commercial
banks, mutual savings banks, savings and loan associations, credit unions, mortgage companies, government
agencies like the Veterans Administration, Farmer's Home)
for a mortgage, you might find a good fixed-rate mortgage
opportunity, but chances are that you'll also come across
other types of "creative financing."

Fixed-Rate Mortgages
The conventional fixed-rate mortgage usually runs for 20
to 30 years, with the interest rate and total amount of
monthly payment constant throughout the life of the loan.
This type of mortgage usually carries the highest interest
rate because it currently puts the greatest long-term risk on
the lender. In today's volatile climate of high interest rates
and inflation, banks are skittish about being committed to
fixed rates for long periods of time. After all, long-term,
low-interest mortgages are the reason many savings and
loans have merged or are on the verge of collapse: they
have been locked into long-term mortgages written at low
rates while the interest rates in general have risen dramatically. In short, the cost of attracting money outstripped the
income that the thrift institutions were able to produce from
the low-interest mortgages they already had made.

While some banks are still willing to offer a fixed-rate
mortgage, the term may be much shorter—three to five
years—with a "balloon payment" at the end. When the
balloon-note mortgage terminates, the borrower has to pay
the outstanding balance or refinance the mortgage. Although such mortgages can include guaranteed refinancing

pegged to when the balloon payment comes due, some lenders have been unwilling to make that guarantee. Do not accept a short-term mortgage with the balloon unless the creditor gives you a guarantee in writing, even at a higher rate.

Most mortgage lenders today charge fees for originating a mortgage—usually between two and four "points," or 2 to 4 percent of the principal amount. Furthermore, most banks require a minimum 20 percent down payment unless a borrower buys mortgage insurance. With this insurance, banks can then lend up to 100 percent of the appraised value of the house.

Adjustable-Rate Mortgages

An adjustable-rate or variable-rate mortgage, as the name implies, carries an interest rate that is readjusted periodically during the life of the loan to reflect the general interest rate levels. Like fixed-interest mortgages, these loans are usually made for 25 or 30 years, but rate adjustments occur at specified intervals—usually every six months, year, 30 months, three years, or five years.

The changes in interest rates generally are tied to some index like the national average mortgage rate for existing homes maintained by the Federal Home Loan Bank Board (which regulates federal savings and loan associations). At each adjustment period, the lender recomputes the monthly payment schedule, depending upon whether the index has gone up or down. The amount of interest-rate change can be limited or "capped," either for each adjustment period or for the life of a loan. (For example, the interest could not change more than one point every six months, or six points over a loan life of 30 years.)

Adjustable-rate mortgages also can be "payment-capped." That is, the interest rate might change frequently, but the monthly payment would remain fixed for longer periods of time. With each rate change, the allocation of payments each month between principal and interest also changes; if the interest rate rises, more of the monthly payment goes to interest; if the rate falls, more goes to principal.

If the interest rate continually moves up in the payment-capped mortgage, your total monthly payment might not be enough to cover the reallocation to a larger amount of interest. When this happens, the uncovered interest would be added into your remaining principal, resulting in a principal that increases, instead of decreasing, over time. Normally, you "amortize" a loan, decreasing your debt in regular installments. In this case, however, you produce "negative amortization." Periodically (perhaps every three to five years), the lender recomputes a new monthly payment based upon the current interest rate level and the borrower's outstanding balance. The fluctuating allocation between principal and interest then continues and accumulates until the next readjustment period. What happens with negative amortization, in effect, is that the borrower opts to borrow more in order to keep the monthly payment constant. Thus, at the end of a term, the increased principal may not be paid off in full, in which case the borrower will have to make a single balloon payment.

The two dangers here are that the chosen interest rate indicator truly reflects market conditions (some lag in favor of the bankers) and that you are sucked into making payments on a property in which you will not be able to gain any equity.

Graduated-Payment Mortgages

Graduated-payment mortgages (GPMs) are designed for home buyers who do not earn enough income to meet current mortgage rates, but who expect to increase their income significantly in the years ahead to accommodate larger mortgage payments.

Offered under a Federal Housing Administration–sponsored program, GPMs help young people buy a house sooner than they ordinarily might be able to do. These mortgages develop into a fixed rate of interest and a constant monthly payment, but not at first. Payments start low and gradually increase for a stated period of time—say, five years—at which time the higher monthly payment remains fixed for the remainder of the term. Because the initial payments are not large enough to cover the interest due, the unpaid interest is added into the outstanding principal, creating negative amortization during the graduation period.

Newer editions of graduated-payment mortgages might carry adjustable interest rates rather than fixed ones. In these cases, the early payment increases are the result of the stated graduation schedule, the same as with the fixed-interest graduated-payment mortgage. But again, uncovered interest is accounted for through negative amortization, and because interest rates can rise, this negative amortization may be higher than in fixed interest cases.

Zero-Rate Mortgages

Zero-rate mortgages are usually designed by developers to attract home buyers who, for one reason or another, cannot qualify for conventional loans or are scared off by high rates. Under these mortgages, a buyer pays just principal, no interest. To compensate for the foregone interest, the developer raises the price of a house and allows the buyer to pay installments over a stated repayment period. Depending upon the length of the loan period, the premium might turn out to be less than the aggregate costs of a conventional mortgage—but there would be no available deductions for interest on the buyer's annual income tax return, a major drawback. You lose one of the most important reasons for home ownership. By accepting a zero-rate mortgage, you are betting that interest rates will remain high and inflation will shoot up again, pushing the market value of your home or co-op above current levels.

Shared Appreciation Mortgages

In the case of a shared appreciation mortgage (SAM), the lender offers the buyer a mortgage at an interest rate that is lower than the prevailing market rate. In exchange, the lender receives a share of the value of a property when the owner sells it. Typically, the interest rate is one third lower than the market rate in exchange for one third of the profit. Naturally, this has become a viable approach for lenders in the present climate of continuous and substantial appreciation in real estate values. In turn, the low interest rates on such mortgages are an obvious attraction for buyers, although it is not clear whether the appreciation payment to a lender upon the sale of a property is deductible as an interest payment. Even if the IRS rules that it is, the overall tax savings for a borrower still might not be as great as they would be with a more conventional higher interest mortgage.

A SAM is usually a better risk for the lender than for the consumer-owner, since this type of mortgage finances only a portion of the original purchase price while the lender's share of the profit is based on 100 percent of the net appreciation when the property is sold or refinanced (it *must* be refinanced if it has not been sold after 10 years).

Second Mortgages

At one time people would look askance if you told them that you were applying for a second mortgage—"You must be in trouble." No more. The writing of second mortgages has grown from a mere "subset" of institutional financing into a burgeoning practice as more and more banks throughout America eagerly enter the field.

Essentially, a second mortgage isn't so much a pure real estate loan as it is a way to borrow money using real estate as collateral. Suppose, for example, you need to pay unexpected medical bills, air condition your house, or put a down payment on a second home. If you have paid your mortgage to $50,000 while the property's value has risen to $150,000, you have built up a $100,000 in equity that you can use as collateral—borrowing against this collateral through a second mortgage.

A second mortgage is an attractive lending device for

banks because of the stability and continuous appreciation of real estate values. It is a higher interest loan than a first mortgage—primarily because the lender takes higher risks. That is, in case the borrower defaults on the loan, the second mortgage lender gets paid only after tax liens and the first mortgage get paid. In spite of these higher interest rates, however, a second mortgage is frequently a viable way to borrow money because it offers longer terms of payment and is easier to get because of the attractiveness and acceptability of real estate as collateral. And there is usually no requirement that your second mortgage be with the same bank as your first.

Owner Financing

While these "creative" types of third-party or institutional financing might open up some options for home buyers, the generally high-interest-rate climate is pushing borrowers toward even more creative mortgage instruments; owner (seller) financing or purchase-money mortgages. Seller financing has long been used in commercial real estate practice, but is now becoming common in residential transactions as well. Under these types of alternative arrangements, the seller "takes back a mortgage"—makes a mortgage loan directly to the buyer, with no bank involved as an intermediary. The seller grants a mortgage for the purchase price of the house (less down payment) and the buyer obtains title to the property, making regular payments to the seller. Purchase-money mortgages frequently are able to offer interest rates below institutional mortgages, mainly because the single seller does not have to cover the higher overhead costs of banks, and sometimes because the seller is eager to make a sale.

There are virtually no rules in owner financing. Payment arrangements can be made through interest plus principal payments; interest-only payments; balloon-note payments—almost any arrangement satisfies the mutual needs of buyer and seller. In some instances, buyers can assume a seller's mortgage, simply by paying the seller an amount equal to the seller's equity and taking over the mortgage payments. Because these existing mortgages are frequently at rates far below those on new mortgages, lenders have recently tried to stop the assumption of mortgages by enforcing the "due-on-sale" clause now contained in many mortgages—this clause requires the balance of the loan to be paid off when the real estate is sold. Nevertheless, court decisions and some state laws may prevent lenders from enforcing due-on-sale clauses in 17 states (Arizona, California, Florida, Georgia, Illinois, Iowa, Michigan, Minnesota, Mississippi, New Mexico, New York, Ohio, Oklahoma, South Carolina, Washington, Arkansas, and Colorado). If you live elsewhere, you might suggest to your state legislator to make it happen.

The variability and creativity of owner financing does not mean that there shouldn't be safeguards for both sides in a purchase-money mortgage. The seller's loan is usually secured by a mortgage that can be enforced in court if the buyer defaults and, in some states, the loan is secured by a deed of trust (which functions like a mortgage).

Whether you approach institutional lenders or seek out owner financing, the name of the real estate borrowing game is to "protect the constant." That is, to keep the total payment of principal and interest each month as stable, predictable, and manageable as possible. In bygone days, we lived for the time we could be free and clear of our mortgage; the old farm used to hold mortgage-burning celebrations. Today we do not necessarily live to pay off the old mortgage, but to perpetuate it—to maintain it at a level of "debt service," or monthly payments, that we can afford.

MAKING COMPARISONS

In keeping with your lookout for a "gentle constant," you should shop for mortgage arrangements that serve your particular budgetary and financial needs. Know your budget and plan ahead: estimate the growth rate of your income and compare it to the possible increases in available adjustable-rate mortgages. Find out what index each lender uses to calculate rate increases—and avoid those indexes based on a lender's own cost of funds. Rather, insist on a mortgage with rate changes based on an index beyond an individual lender's control (such as the national average mortgage rate or the six-month Treasury bill rate). Ask lenders for examples of how the index has moved recently to check its volatility. And insist that lenders give you a realistic disclosure of how much your monthly payments might vary if interest were to rise or fall by one point or five points—what's the worst possible scenario?

When you compare interest rate–capped mortgages versus payment-capped mortgages, consider your particular needs. With a rate cap, your monthly payments may be larger, but will cover the interest rate increases in an adjustable-rate mortgage and you will probably pay less total interest. Your choice rests in what you need. With payment-capped mortgage, you would be able to take tax deductions for the additional interest paid, but you would accumulate negative amortization, which might become a problem if you wanted to sell the property. On the other hand, if you expected to be in the house for a relatively short time, you wouldn't be concerned with the amount of interest you would accumulate over 20 or 30 years.

Your mortgage decisions, then, depend not only on how much you can afford, but on how you intend to live: your money *and* your life.

Chapter Nine

What
to Do
When You're
in Trouble

As we've seen in Chapter 5 ("shaping your loan application"), the key to building good credit while keeping out of
trouble is to budget your debt just as you budget your cash.
Nevertheless, many Americans—with an assemblage of
credit cards, charge cards, auto loans, mortgages, and
overdraft checking privileges—unwittingly find themselves
overloaded with debt today. In fact, if we spread out evenly
the nation's $340 billion in consumer debt, we would find
that each household owed an average of $4,000 (excluding
mortgage obligations) to various consumer creditors.

It used to take years to get deeply in debt. Now we see
people in their early twenties—both married and single—
unable to pay their monthly bills. For many of them, the
problem is not one of credit gluttony or whimsy; few people
are really trying to beat the system. More often, the debt
scenario comes about quite unsuspectingly: a couple goes
along easily with the flow of the system, using its credit to
the limit, being extended more credit, and then using that to
the limit. Everything is fine until something happens. A
two-income family, for example, becomes a one-income

182

family when the husband loses his job or the wife goes on maternity leave. Or there is a serious illness or accident, an unexpected expense. Suddenly, the "house of credit cards" falls.

Even if you are not faced with a traumatic event, there are a number of early signs that can warn you when you are in trouble. Your debt (excluding mortgage) is unreasonably higher than 20 percent of your take-home pay—the conventional rule-of-thumb for credit manageability. You have been making the minumum monthly payments and still find your total debt mounting. You are getting increasingly belligerent dunning letters from creditors and threats of legal action from collection agencies. Not only are you apprehensive about paying next month's bills, you're afraid to answer the phone and can't bear to look at the mail. Fear becomes paranoia. It looms over you as a moral issue even more than a financial problem. You are being judged as inadequate and irresponsible. You avoid your creditors and the longer you refuse to communicate the harder it is for you to act.

FACE THE FACTS

If you find yourself in this kind of credit trouble, it's important to recognize it, face it. It is not a moral issue. It's nearly always a problem of timing: what you're paying back is simply increasing at a more rapid rate of inflation than what you're bringing in. It's not the end of the world, and you can handle it. Furthermore, your troubles are not unique in your creditor's eyes either. The world of credit has gotten so sophisticated that loans and other credit extensions are treated essentially as statistical gambles, with provisions for projected loan losses added right into the original cost of making you the loan. In the past few years alone, the consumer debt scene has changed drastically, according to a study by the Budget and Credit Counseling Service (BuCCS) in New York City. Whereas the overwhelming majority of people seeking credit counseling used to be poor and uneducated, today the threat of debt default is squarely a middle-class problem: 33 percent of those who request counseling from BuCCS are college graduates; 74 percent hold skilled or professional jobs; and 40 percent earn more than $21,000 a year.

So you are not unique in your troubles nor are you morally bereft. You must shake off shame and guilt; being guilt-ridden doesn't unshackle you from being debt-ridden. This is just a temporary setback for you—a problem of logistics and timing—but you must do something about it while there is still "smoke and no flame." It's a question of opening the windows, so to speak, and getting rid of the smoke by communicating with your creditors, reworking your budget, and righting your credit life.

The first step in working your way out of trouble is take written inventory and make a list of all your creditors and obligations: bank loans, car loans, finance company loans, mortgage, credit cards, charge cards, department store cards, utility bills, medical bills, and so forth. Next to each creditor put the account number and phone number; how much is owed on a monthly basis and in total; and how far behind you are in your payments. Add up the totals: how much you owe each month and how much you owe altogether. Your goal here is to sit down in a clear-headed way and rework your budget and payment schedules in a way that satisfies your creditors, meets your present financial capacity, and protects your creditworthiness.

THAT FIRST PHONE CALL

Before you actually wring out the numbers, you should call each of your creditors. (The credit representative or office to call is usually listed on your bill or reminder notices.) This is best done in the middle of the month, two weeks before you're due to make your next rash of payments—you should be well aware that the upcoming payments may be impossible to make if you've heeded your "trouble-alert system." This first phone call to the creditor is important for three reasons:

1. *It establishes a dialogue with the creditor, and it's important that YOU initiate this contact.* By reaching out you demonstrate your good faith, your intent to pay. You will get a more sympathetic ear by making the first call, and as long as you keep up the dialogue, the creditor will rarely do anything precipitous. Communication saves face for a credit representative: when asked by a supervisor how your account is going, the best thing he or she can report (next to actually getting the money) is, "I'm in touch with the account and we're working out a payment schedule."

2. *Making the call early prevents your account from being sent to a collection agency or into litigation.* Your creditor doesn't want your account to go into collection—he loses income when he charges off your account and pays an agency to take you on. Nor is it in your best interest to end up in collection—when this happens, making deals to gain time will be much tougher to do. So when you make the first call, be sure to speak to a representative with the authority to pull out or intercept your account from the computerized collection process.

3. *The phone call is critical in assuring your continued creditworthiness.* The creditor should think that you are obsessive about your credit reputation—it's just as important as the actual paying back of your debts. Get hold of your credit bureau reports beforehand to see which creditors, if any, are listing you as "slow." You recognize that good credit is *voluntary* paying, not being coerced. While you want to renegotiate a payment schedule, you don't want to be reported as a slow payer. You need to talk to your creditors about how they report to credit bureaus because your primary concern is to protect your good credit name as you pay them back.

When you make that first phone call, proceed in a direct, truthful manner. For example:

Hello, Mr. Lorry, this is Mr. Carton calling about my credit card account number _____ . I need your help. I'm experiencing some financial problems at the moment—my budget has been hit by inflation even harder than I had anticipated [you could mention other specifics here, if appropriate, like sudden large and unexpected expenses].

I really believe that my problem is one of mistiming, and I need the next month to sit down and redo my family budget. I won't be able to make the next payment but I want to give you my complete assurance that I will be paying you and all my creditors back. I don't believe in bankruptcy. My credit is very important to me and I want to demonstrate that I can handle it myself—it's better for me, and it's better for you.

What I'm asking from you is to help me out by giving me some time to talk things over with my family; work out a careful budget for these new economic circumstances; and then come back to you with a proposal for a firm repayment plan that both of us can live with. Of course, I've stopped using credit and won't use it again until I'm back on my feet. In the meantime, I'd like to give you a call once a week to keep you apprised of my progress. If you would like to get in touch with me, feel free to call me at home between the hours of _____ and _____ .

"Frequent and intimate contact": that, as one lender put it, is working well with creditors. Make them participate in your struggle; involve them in supporting what they helped create—a collaboration between debtor and creditor aimed at finding a satisfactory arrangement to repay your debt. The relationship with your creditor should be developed just as it was with the banker: through the power of trust. Communicate attitudes, needs, facts, and feelings. Be hopeful. Give the credit representatives something to support and something to report to their supervisor; otherwise, they will just send your account into collection. And if they feel that they can't make a deal with you, you're talking to the wrong person—move on or move up to their supervisor.

THE ORDER OF REPAYMENT

There is a fairly commonsensical order to dealing with creditors: (1) finance companies, followed by (2) utilities, (3) department stores, retail stores, and oil companies, (4) credit and charge card companies, (5) banks extending consumer credit, and (6) mortgage lenders. In a sense, finance companies are in a class by themselves—they bug you the most even though they're usually the best secured (through forms of collateral like wage assignments). It's just in their nature: their management is measured by how well they collect on delinquencies, so they are more acutely aware of the time value of money. In contrast, other creditors generally should be dealt with in an inverse order to the extent that they're secured. That is, your utilities—"products" that you use before you pay for them—are the least secured and should be taken care of first to alleviate the creditors' anxieties, not to mention your own. You have to protect these essential services from being cut off because, without them, your family can't continue living, let alone straighten out your debt. Mortgage companies, on the other hand, are heavily secured and are easiest to deal with. They're generally not worried about your debt going into default, and, unless you have a small mortgage outstanding, these companies would rather work out any sort of repayment instead of going through the complicated legal process of foreclosure.

When dealing with your utilities—electricity, water, gas, oil, and phone service—make sure these creditors know you want them to continue with you during your "recasting period." There are no formulas, and local managers have a good bit of discretion in negotiating repayment schedules—usually based upon each customer's past payment habits.

The phone company, for example, rates each customer from A to D, sending payment reminders to Cs and Ds sooner than to As or Bs. If a person has a good payment record and initiates the negotiation (again, demonstrating good faith), "he doesn't have a worry in the world," according to a Bell spokesman. A common arrangement is for the current bills to be paid in full while past accumulated debt is spread over a period of months. Generally, utilities will "go out six months," allowing the customer to pay one sixth of his past debt each month while he keeps current.

When you call on department stores and other companies with "single-purpose cards," remember that the goal of their collection departments is to bring your account current so that you can go back into their stores or stations to shop. They may freeze your card after you are one month in arrears, but they will be eager to work out a repayment schedule with you, especially if you contact them first and relieve them of the task of calling you to find out what's going on. With stores, you have the edge of personalization: you can walk in and meet with the collection manager (do it during the day; at night there is usually a part-time clerk). Most collection managers simply want you to be straightforward, sincere. After you pay off your debt, these single-purpose card companies usually will reconsider opening your account—a good way to reestablish your credit life once you're back on your feet. Check your credit bureau reports to make sure that any negative items about slow payments are removed as part of your repayment agreement.

When dealing with credit cards (bank cards like VISA or MasterCard) or charge cards (travel and expense cards like American Express, Diners Club, Carte Blanche) emphasize that you're not going to buy or borrow any more until your account is settled. If you work out a deal with the collection clerk or manager, you're usually allowed to keep your card—but if they insist that you return it, send it back. Under these circumstances, you would have trouble using it anyway, since you'd be listed in "the book"—the file of charge card delinquencies. Being placed in the book or on "watch lists" is something you want to avoid, so it's important to intercept the process, especially in situations where you've exceeded your credit card limit—get to them soon. Charge card collectors generally differ from credit card collectors in what they ask for to bring your account current: credit card collectors may require collection of any minimum past due payments while charge card collectors may ask for past bills paid in full. Nevertheless, charge card collectors are fairly flexible in working out arrangements (go as high as you can, to a collection manager, if possible). If you have been a cardholder for several years, with few previous problems, your card probably will be suspended, rather than canceled, during the time your account is being settled.

Each time you talk to a collection department—whether it be a charge card company or a bank—your contact is noted and the nature of the conversation recorded on your three-by-five delinquency card (or, more frequently these days, entries are made into a computer terminal). While many companies make a point of putting the same collector on a customer's file until it's paid up, it's a good idea to make a point of this yourself. The more the credit representative knows about you and the more you talk, the easier it will be to move through your "recasting" period with minimum anxiety—and the easier it will be to reestablish your normal credit relationships with these lenders. Personalization is particularly important in situations made sensitive by the presence of collateral: cars, boats, houses. Even though auto loans and boat loans are no longer secured loans in states like New York (no longer do banks have the power to repossess the debtor's purchase), lenders may or may not go for a judgment in cases of delinquency. It boils down to the economic reality of individual cases, and when you fall into trouble you leave yourself open to a lawsuit.

And even though mortgage lenders may let you put off

payments for three months, the inability to make monthly mortgage payments is usually a sign to them of serious debt problems—so you should take the time to visit them and assure them that their loan is not in jeopardy. In these situations, consider a repayment arrangement similar to your utilities plan, where you continue to make current payments while spreading the past due debt over several months until you're up to date. The "bottom line," then, in working out of trouble with creditors is not just paying back the debts; it's *how* you handle the payments that demonstrate to your creditors your essential creditworthiness.

REEVALUATING YOUR BUDGET

Now, before you can go back to your creditors with the actual details of each repayment plan, you've got to go back to your budget. If you've prepared a budget in the manner we've described in Chapter 5, when you applied for a loan, clearly something has gone awry in your projection. You've got to sit down again and recalculate your income and outflow: take out all your monthly receipts; itemize your necessary expenses and subtract them from your income—this amount is what you may allocate to creditors over the next three months. You may need more than three months to realign your credit life, but proceed on a 90-day to 90-day basis; it's a manageable hunk of time, and after the first period you can reexamine your situation and bump up or reduce your payment as necessary.

Reevaluating your budget may require a close scrutiny of each item, line by line. Where do you really spend your money? What needs are fulfilled by each expense? What things are really necessities? What are recurring expenses? Could you be making money out of your avocations or interests? Finding the answers to these questions means working things out with your family—experimenting to see what works best in cutting down expenses, perhaps implementing some changes in lifestyles. Your payments to creditors should be calculated on a pro rata basis, in proportionate amounts, in accordance with how much you owe each creditor. Once you determine the payment schedule for the first three months, it's important to stick to it. Don't make pie-in-the-sky promises, because if you fail to come through, you will have lost your relationship of trust and collaboration and, most likely, your creditor will toss your account into collection. Even if your creditor objects that your proposed payments are too small, stick close to them if that's what you really feel you can afford to pay. The creditor should realize that it's important for the payment schedule to stick, but if there is too much protest at your arrived amounts, you should invoke your own "power of morality": "I'm trying to be fair to all my creditors and get out of debt as soon as possible. Why won't you help me out?"

CAREFUL USE OF COUNSELORS

You may find, as you sit down to rework your budget, that you are overwhelmed by a complicated debt situation, or that you have other emotional or psychological problems that contribute to your debt situation—you might be a "spendaholic" or a compulsive gambler. While it's important to go through the process of budgeting and contacting creditors, it may be that you need the additional mental discipline of organizations such as Overspenders Anonymous, Debtors Anonymous, or financial counseling groups like the Consumer Credit Counseling Service (CCCS) or the Budget and Credit Counseling Service (BuCCS).

CCCS and BuCCS represent two basic types of counseling services, although there are many similar organizations across the country that vary tremendously in size and quality. With some 200 branches nationwide, CCCS is supported by a mixture of credit granting institutions like banks and finance companies. It offers a free analysis of your income and expenses, as well as guidance on credit use, de-

signed to show the consumer where to pare down expenses
and balance a budget. CCCS also provides (for a monthly
charge not exceeding $12) a debt management program that
usually reorganizes the consumer's debt by putting together
a schedule of reduced payments to creditors—the basic approach outlined earlier in this chapter. BuCCS, a New York
City–based organization, is supported by community
groups like the United Way, in addition to foundations, corporations, and financial institutions. Its programs are totally free, ranging from credit and budget counseling to debt
management and renegotiation. Counselors from BuCCS
may offer to call up your creditors on your behalf: "We try
to find out what's fair," says Robert Edelstein, director of
strategic research for BuCCS. "We act in the interest of
both parties; debts are usually incurred in good faith and
should be paid off in good faith."

Critics of CCCS say that because it is supported by creditors and, in fact, returns a percentage of the monies received through its debt management program to creditors,
it runs the risk of becoming a "glorified collection agency."
(Other counseling services are considered "feeders" into
main lines like insurance companies or legal and tax services.) Critics of BuCCS, in turn, say that it favors debtors
over creditors and acts as a "bankruptcy mill"—although
Edelstein maintains that in many cases it steers consumers
away from bankruptcy by teaching them what credit is
about and what their rights and options are. Many counseling organizations recommend cutting your credit cards in
two as a means of "biting the bullet" and getting hold of
your debt. But in all but the extreme cases—where a consumer is a spendaholic, completely unable to control his or
her compulsive spending—destroying the credit you have
built is little more than regressive symbolism. If you're that
worried about succumbing to your impulses, put your cards
in a safe-deposit box until you get back on your feet—that's
symbolic enough.

BEWARE OF REFINANCING

In the course of reworking your budget—with or without outside counseling—you may find that refinancing or consolidation loans are a viable way to restructure your personal loans or mortgage and gain the time you need to even out your credit burdens. Refinancing agreements are ones where you go back to a creditor and reborrow the outstanding balance of your loan over a longer period of time, but usually at a higher interest rate. For example, if you have a $6,000 auto loan with the General Motors Acceptance Corporation, to be paid over 36 months at an interest rate of 13 percent, and you're 18 months into the loan, you might agree to repay the remaining $3,000 balance over another 36-month term at a rate of 15 percent. Auto loan grantors seem especially accustomed to and amenable to working with unexpected financial problems with customers by refinancing their loans—but again, *your* initiative in contacting them as soon as possible is important.

Similarly, consolidation loans (usually made with finance companies) are ones where you "borrow long to pay short"—the bank or finance company offers to pay your bills now and you, in turn, agree to repay the company over a long period of time—at a higher rate of interest, of course. The obvious advantage of a consolidation loan is the convenience of paying one creditor that takes care of the rest. The disadvantage is that this type of loan is way too expensive—you're borrowing against the expectation of higher future income—and it commits you to a long period of indebtedness. Some customers end up continuously rewriting and consolidating loans for 10 or 15 years, paying more in interest than principal. Furthermore, the chances of a debt consolidation loan actually helping you in the long run depends upon whether you take the time to evaluate your budget and reorganize your credit and cash habits.

Refinancing or debt consolidation are expensive alternatives; still, they are useful in giving you a "target." That is, if a finance company offers you a debt consolidation loan of $220 per month (your current obligations are $345 monthly), now, at least, you have a target dollar amount to shoot for in devising your own debt repayment plan with creditors. Your goal is to arrive at a monthly payment that equals the lower level offered by the finance company without pinning you down to such a long-term obligation. You may find that the convenience of dealing with only one creditor like the finance company is worth the extended payout. Nevertheless, it's important to try to put your credit life in order yourself—for your own sense of financial control, maturity, and creditworthiness.

In the commercial world, banks have created "workout specialists" who step in and help reorganize debtors when business loans become delinquent. It's frequently a traumatic experience for the borrower and should serve as a lesson to you, the consumer: while counselors, finance companies, and banks can help you get back in line, it's usually best to be your own "workout specialist" if you can.

HANDLING THE COLLECTION AGENCY
Even if you take charge of your workout period, it's possible that some negotiation with creditors may not proceed smoothly and that an account may end up with a collection agency. Here, the going gets a bit tougher, but your basic procedure is the same. Take the initiative. Call first, don't wait for the agency to call. Some collection agencies are so sophisticated that they will call you with a computerized message that will ask you questions about why you haven't paid your bill and when you plan to pay—fully programmed to respond to an array of answers you might provide and to close the "dialogue" with your agreement to pay. Short-circuit the computer by calling first. Computers are designed to take planned, overt action, so if you surprise the collector with an unexpected phone call you effec-

tively eliminate the humiliation of having to explain yourself to a machine.

While you want to initiate the contact with a collection
agency, don't worry about establishing the same type of
cordial relationship you might have with a creditor. Collection agencies are in the business of collecting money—fast.
They're not pleasant by nature. They may keep within the
bounds of the law, but the basic premise of the collection
industry is that "he who acts toughest gets paid fastest."
Collectors are like high-pressure salesmen who try to control you, cajole you, oblige you, and "close you"—get you
to pay up now. Occasionally, they may try to bend the rules
by harassing or threatening you. You don't have to stand
for that. Under the Fair Debt Collection Practices Act, ef-
fected in March 1978, you have a good deal of protection
from abusive collectors.

• Collectors may not "harass, oppress or abuse a person
in connection with the collection of a debt." This means
that they may *not* threaten you with violence; use obscene
language; publicize the debt (except to a consumer reporting agency—and if the debt is in dispute, this, too, must be
reported to the agency); or annoy you with repetitive or
anonymous phone calls.

• When communicating with you, collectors may *not* call
you at an inconvenient or unusual time or place. (Generally, a convenient time is assumed to be between 8:00 A.M.
and 9:00 P.M.) Debt collectors may not call you if they know
you are represented by an attorney (unless the attorney
fails to respond or gives them permission to speak directly
with you). They may not call you at work if it is known that
your employer prohibits such calls; and they may not communicate with any third parties without your consent or the
permission of an appropriate court—the communication is
solely for the purpose of locating you. Under that circum-
stance, a collector must identify himself or herself (but not
his or her employer, unless asked); only tell people that the

purpose is to contact you, not that you owe any money; not use a postcard or put anything on an envelope that identifies the debt collector; and, in most cases, not talk to any person about you more than once.

• Debt collectors *may not* use any false or deceptive statements or practices. Specifically, they cannot *falsely imply* that they represent a government agency or impersonate an attorney or a credit bureau; nor can they falsely imply that you committed a crime or send you papers that simulate or represent forms (such as summonses) as legal when they are not. Collectors cannot tell you that any action will be taken against you that cannot *legally* be taken. And if you do not want to be contacted further by a collection agency, tell them in writing—and they can no longer do so except to tell you that there will be no further contact or that some specific action will be taken (if the collector usually takes such action).

Clearly, then, you are armed with a bundle of rights as a debtor, but it is still better to act first than to wait. By calling first, you show good faith: you obviate the need of a collection agency to call around, trying to find you, either overtly or inadvertently smearing your credit reputation. If you call the agency and *tell* them to consult with you on your home phone between certain hours, the likelihood is much greater that they will not try to embarrass you at work, claiming that they had no reason to know that your employer prohibits you from receiving such communication. Don't be abusive. Be truthful and direct with your collector; you are always protected by truth. Ask the collector if the agency is a member of the American Collectors Association, a trade organization whose members are obligated to follow a code of ethics and operations. After you have negotiated a settlement, write the agency a letter of agreement, stipulating the points of your payment plan and procedures—a good practice in dealing with both creditors and collectors.

If you find that, in spite of your efforts to negotiate, the collector tries to "strong arm" you, contact the local office of consumer protection or the regional office of the Federal Trade Commission—and tell your collector and his client that you have done so. If you're unsure, check with the FTC to make sure that the collection agency is covered by the Fair Debt Collection Practices Act—it applies generally to "third-party" collectors, not to banks and other businesses that collect their own accounts under their own corporate name. Many states also have their own debt collection laws, so check with your state attorney general's office to determine your rights under state law.

STOP THE OUTFLOW

One much-overlooked way to raise cash when you're in trouble is to stop making any and all payments using credit and charge cards. If you sit down and realize that you are $3,000 behind in payments and you take home $3,000 a month, it comes down to eliminating one month's worth of expenses. One way is to "borrow a month"—tell all your creditors that you will not be making payments this month, but that you will be getting back to them to work out a payment plan (see next chapter). That's a relatively straightforward approach.

A more extreme response is to cut down dramatically on your cost of living. Take a cue from International Harvestor, which no longer buys personal stationery for its executives, or Lee Iacocca of Chrysler who slashed his operating expenses in half. We sometimes need extremists to show us the way out of extravagant addictions. A personal friend of mine who went through an expensive divorce settlement and found himself getting further and further behind, living the high life, finally came to his senses and decided to eliminate or cut down on these frills until his income could cover them: cab fares, shoeshines, manicures, laundered shirts, housekeeper, bar tabs, hotel rooms, drugs, cigarettes, long-distance phone calls, lottery tickets, and bets.

The point is that you can create credit by reducing your

normal expenses, thereby increasing your net income.

Finally, if you're really in trouble and don't think there is any way out, consider bankruptcy. There are two ways to file for personal bankruptcy—under Chapter 7 or Chapter 13 of the Federal Bankruptcy Act of 1978. Chapter 7, a "straight" bankruptcy, requires debtors to liquidate their assets (after certain exemptions are taken—for example, equity in a house of up to $7,500 and in a car of up to $1,200) and give the proceeds to their creditors. Once this is done, a debtor is considered completely debt-free, no matter how large the gap was between the liquidation payments and the amount owed to creditors. Chapter 13 provides for a debt repayment plan approved by a bankruptcy court under which the debtor usually pays back a percentage of the money owed on unsecured debt over a period of three years, extendable to five years. This alternative is available to anyone with a regular income who has unsecured debts of less than $100,000 and secured debts of less than $350,000. Typical legal fees for bankruptcy proceedings can range upward from $500, and once a debtor has filed for bankruptcy, he can't file again for six years.

Bankruptcy is the last avenue you should take to stop the "hemorrhaging" of runaway debt. Unless something has happened to permanently cripple your earning power, you should avoid bankruptcy like the plague—because that's what it will be to your credit future. A bankruptcy will remain in your credit bureau files for up to 10 years. That effectively destroys your creditworthiness, although you may be able to reestablish your credit after successfully completing a Chapter 13 repayment plan.

Your good credit name is too valuable to lose to bankruptcy. Heed your "trouble-alert" system when its warns you that you're getting too deeply in debt. It's always easier to negotiate with creditors when you've caught the problem early. When your credit life has been knocked down, you can always get back on your feet—but it's a lot harder if you've been knocked out cold.

Chapter Ten

Creating
the Power
of Credit

CREDIT IS NOT A BIRTHRIGHT AUTOMATICALLY BESTOWED UPON reaching adulthood or dispensed because you come from a good family, have rich relatives, or are sitting on a lot of money in the bank. Credit is created by becoming involved: you have to reach out and earn it. This is not to say that there are no wily ways to work credit wonders overnight. It's just that your success in creating and using the enormous power of credit requires a certain amount of work. Rest assured that your initiative and diligence in choosing among your many credit opportunities will be rewarded by a richer life.

The word "credit" originally comes from the Latin word *credo*, which literally means *I believe*. In essence, credit involves believability or credibility—a sense of trust. Consider trust for a moment: you do not accord trust to someone you don't know, have no sense of what his or her values are, or how these values relate to you. Trust is not a static absolute, born whole and inviolate. It is an emotional bond that gathers strength in degrees through the successful interaction between two or more people. A friend to

199

whom you would have no qualms lending $50 suddenly be-
comes suspect when he or she asks to borrow $5,000. Yet
that same request would not be considered extreme if you
were in the habit of loaning to each other from time to time
$1,000 or $2,000.

Just as trust is gained over time, likewise credit. And yet,
while past actions demonstrate that you are a person of
your word who can be trusted to honor a commitment, your
present behavior must also be seen as consistent, or at least
in keeping with the logical good sense of enhancement, in
order to confirm your good stead. Usually, good credit is
self-perpetuating once in hand. You are assumed to continue to be a good credit risk, but the ultimate validation
comes when you prove yourself by fulfilling that obligation.
Credit is therefore kinetic; it is continually in a state of active appraisal. The problems that arise concerning credit
are usually connected with measuring it or posting present
and future limits based on past performance—or the lack of
credit based on other people's perceptions.

OTHER GROUND RULES

In general, the more often you successfully execute your
credit obligations, the more creditworthy or trusting you
become over time. Credit, like trust, becomes a recognized
part of your personality. Trusted friends introduce you to
their friends, and your persona grows. While the frequency
of competent credit activity and the length of time you have
been engaged in such transactions are the key elements to
creating an impeccable credit standing, there are two natural caveats to keep in mind. First, you can overdo "proving" your credit ability. Of course, it's gratifying to qualify
for a line of credit with a dozen cards and other grantors.
But if your *potential* line of credit creeps up to exceed 20 or
25 percent or your net income, you may wind up having
trouble qualifying for a loan from a bank or other financial
services company at a rate more reasonable than credit

card financing charges. It doesn't matter that you haven't exercised or drawn upon a significant percentage of that line of credit. The next potential creditor is free to assume (and often operates by explicit internal guidelines to assume) that your entire potential of what you can spend on credit will be used during the course of repaying your requested loan, thus constricting the reasonable likelihood of meeting any additional obligations.

Second, good credit experience ages quickly while a bad credit transaction seems to hang over you forever. We have discussed earlier how credit bureaus tend to keep negative credit experience longer than good accounts; for as long as seven years (10 years for bankruptcy), one poor performance can legally continue to cloud your present and future credit potential. When it comes to demonstrating your fiscal trust in positive terms, however, the lender's typical attitude is: "What have you done for us lately?" The paid-up loan for your second child's delivery five years ago was commendable but times have changed, and your potential lender wants to see some current evidence of your creditworthiness. If you haven't used credit for five, or sometimes even three, years or more, your credit standing becomes a question mark. Once upon a time does not make you consistent, stable, and therefore trustworthy.

THE NEW RULES

The new rules of consumer credit, as detailed in the preceding pages, will help you overcome these and other impediments. They amount to your recognition that the computerized and otherwise mechanized methods of determining your supposed level of creditworthiness are inadequate. To ensure that your true personal and unique credit abilities are accorded recognition, you must involve yourself in the credit granting process beyond the mere execution of forms. One of the most significant messages we can offer is the importance of personalizing your request for credit. Your credit message should never be inert; safe delivery usually cannot be entrusted to the mail.

Also, the formulas that creditors cling to, making matrices of us, can be disregarded. As long as you understand all of the costs involved and are convinced that you have the wherewithal to make good on your word, you should not be deterred by going over some set credit spending limit. Lending ratios are stupid; they are predicated on ideas that no longer apply across the mass of humanity—if ever, in fact, they did. Their assumptions frequently do not jibe with your reality—you may have decided, for example, that you don't need life insurance anymore; or that it makes more sense for you to lease rather than to buy certain items. A significant amount of your living expenses, including entertainment, may be picked up by your employer. In short, you should not allow yourself to be pegged into a niche based on creditors homogenizing vast amounts of consumer data.

What you elect to do with your borrowed funds is one thing—how you plan to pay it back is another. You should not be worried about whether you are entitled to credit, you should concern yourself with its cost and how you can pay it back most comfortably. Your budget is everything in determining creditworthiness, not whether you fit into someone else's old mold of success.

CREDIT FOR CREDIT'S SAKE

It is perfectly reasonable to state that among your primary reasons for applying for credit is your desire to establish a good credit history. As long as you also mention that you recognize the value of the product or services and anticipate using it for the foreseeable future, there should be no stigma attached to starting off your credit life. In fact, you might want to add that you consider it essential to start off on the right foot with credit so that there is little doubt that you will pay your bills promptly. Credit managers and staff should recognize and respond to this line of reasoning. They also realize that a credit rejection most likely will result in the loss of a potential or current customer. Stress the fact that you have used their services on a cash basis in the past where it is applicable.

GETTING MORE CREDIT

The standards necessary to qualify for additional credit once you have opened an account are often arbitrary and unrealistically posted way out in the future. Again, the best method for accelerating your level of credit is through personal intervention.

A first-year lawyer employed in a firm recently mentioned that she wanted to have her credit limit raised from $500 to $1,000 on her VISA card because during the Christmas season she spent more and wound up anxious about carrying around cash. Considering her steady income and good record paying back the $500 balance, we told her to make an appointment with her banker to discuss it. After finally resolving a scheduling problem because she commuted to work and was generally unavailable to meet during normal business hours (they arranged a meeting on a bank holiday), her request was quickly approved.

She believes that her persistence and interest in a personal meeting were the deciding factors. After repeated phone calls to reschedule their meeting, she became more than an account number. Yet she felt that it was also important that she did not immediately state that she wanted her VISA credit limit raised. Instead, since she was starting out in a career and already had an account there, she said she was interested in developing a good banking relationship and wanted to discuss a number of financial services. At the meeting, the banker pushed the wonders of an Individual Retirement Account and she listened politely. Finally, the young lawyer said that she might very well be interested in establishing an IRA in the near future, but that her more

pressing need was raising the limit because of her situation.
Done.

THE BIG PICTURE

To be sure, exercising your credit ability has its own cost.
Rates for borrowed funds range all over the lot, from the
insignificant to the exorbitant, so it is essential to compare
before signing. The financial services industry is one of the
fastest growing segments of the U.S. economy. While ex-
citing and viable new credit opportunities are literally coming onto the market every day, hucksters and con artists are
taking advantage of consumer confusion. Beware.

Meanwhile, economists and financial analysts continue
to preach about the inflation dangers of consumer credit as
if we should be issued child-proof caps on our credit. Consumer debt is not inflationary in itself, despite the hypocrit-
ical cant now in vogue. What is inflationary is buying goods
at any price; this misconduct applies equally or perhaps
more to businesses that in turn try to raise their prices to
consumers.

THE LAST WORD

A successful credit relationship can be more than satisfactory. It is a validation of your character and your creditor's judgment, and is the basis for a bond. Among social
peers, it's called friendship: a mutual demonstration of trust
and caring about each other's well-being and enhancement.
You respect and enjoy each other, and there is honor in
that. No, we are not suggesting that you swap mantras or
buy vacation property with your creditor. That's getting too
cozy. But if you recognize that credit is inextricably bound
in very human emotions of trust, honor, and even faith at
times, you can begin to cater to those needs without being
unfairly drawn in or duped.

Perhaps the most powerful psychic compensation that

credit offers is hope. When you create credit options in a sensible and unsullied fashion, a vista emerges. You have more control over your life because you are prepared for the future with all of its opportunities. You can dream with your feet on the ground. And if and when you make that great leap of faith, you are taking off from a platform with a solid support system and cheering section.

Summarizing Your

Credit Rights

THE EQUAL CREDIT OPPORTUNITY ACT GIVES YOU THE RIGHT TO:

- find out the reasons for credit denial
- receive credit in your own name
- refuse to answer questions about childbearing plans or birth control practices
- have equal consideration of all credit criteria, including income, between the sexes in determining creditworthiness
- have alimony, child support, and separate maintenance considered as any other income

The Fair Credit Reporting Act gives you the right to:

- know what is in your credit bureau file
- correct any errors and have them recorded in a timely fashion
- enter a statement into your file in the event of a dispute telling your side of the story
- have any corrected or amended information sent out to all creditors and employers who received your credit file within the last six months to two years

The Truth-in-Lending Act gives you the right to:

• a complete, written explanation of both the annual percentage rate (APR) being charged for any credit transaction, and the total dollar amount of the transaction, except for mortgages

The Fair Credit Billing Act gives you the right to:

• withhold payment on any disputed portion of a billing until the creditor resolves the dispute
• receive acknowledgment from a creditor within 30 days
• have the creditor resolve a dispute within two full billing cycles

The Fair Debt Collection Practices Act gives you the right to:

• receive verification from the debt collector of the amount that you owe
• not to be harassed or threatened by a debt collector

Where to Push
the Up Button

IF YOU NEED FURTHER HELP OR BECOME INVOLVED IN A DISPUTE, consider consulting with the consumer affairs office of the company involved, the Better Business Bureau, your local or state consumer protection agency, or one of the following federal enforcement agencies listed below.

For complaints involving retail stores, department stores, small loan and finance companies, public utilities, state credit unions, credit or charge card companies, or government lending programs, contact:

Consumer Inquiries
Federal Trade Commission
Washington, D.C. 20580
(202) 523-3598

For complaints about a nationally chartered bank (National or N.A. will be a part of its name), contact:

Consumer Affairs Division
Comptroller of the Currency
Washington, D.C. 20219
(202) 447-1600

For complaints against a state-chartered bank that is a member of the Federal Reserve System, contact:

Consumer Affairs Division
Board of Governors of the
Federal Reserve System
Washington, D.C. 20551
(202) 452-3693

For complaints concerning a state-chartered bank insured by the Federal Deposit Insurance Corporation, but *not* a member of the Federal Reserve System, contact:

Consumer Affairs Division
Federal Deposit Insurance Corporation
Washington, D.C. 20429
(202) 389-4767 or
(800) 424-5488 (toll-free)

For problems regarding a federally chartered or federally insured savings and loan, contact:

Consumer & Civil Rights Office
Federal Home Loan Bank Board
Washington, D.C. 20552
(202) 377-6237

For complaints about a federally chartered or insured credit union, contact:

Consumer Affairs Division
National Credit Union Administration
Washington, D.C. 20456
(202) 357-1080

For problems regarding stocks and bond brokers and dealers, contact:

Securities and Exchange Commission
Washington, D.C. 20549
(202) 272-7430

For complaints about airlines, contact:

Director, Bureau of Enforcement
Civil Aeronautics Board
1825 Connecticut Avenue, N.W.
Washington, D.C. 20428
(202) 673-5930

For complaints concerning small business investment companies, contact:

U.S. Small Business Administration
1441 L Street, N.W.
Washington, D.C. 20416
(202) 655-4000

For problems relating to Federal Land Banks, Federal Land Bank Associations, Federal Intermediate Credit Banks, and Production Credit Associations, contact:

Consumer Affairs Division
Farm Credit Administration
490 L'Enfant Plaza, S.W.
Washington, D.C. 20578
(202) 775-2195

If you are unsure which agency has jurisdiction over your credit problem, contact:

Division of Consumer Affairs
Board of Governors of the Federal Reserve System
Washington, D.C. 20551
(202) 452-3946

Finally, complaints against *all* kinds of creditors may be referred to:

General Litigation Section
Civil Rights Division
Department of Justice
Washington, D.C. 20530
(202) 633-4713

Major U.S.
Credit Bureaus

Below we have compiled a list of major credit bureaus across the U.S., the first such list to be published. If you have been denied credit within the last thirty days, you are entitled to a free look at your credit bureau report including verbal disclosure. While most credit bureaus contacted will give you a written copy of your report, they are not required to do so by law, and you can still be charged for a written copy, except where prohibited, even if you have been rejected for credit. In case you have not been rejected for credit, the cost of a written copy and/or credit interview are listed in most instances. Also listed are the costs for adding trade lines or credit references to your report.

ALABAMA

Credit Bureau, Inc. Anniston
1316 Noble Street
Anniston, 36202
(205) 237-5484
$7.00 for credit report with no
  rejection.

Credit Bureau, Inc. Dothan
Colonial Square Executive Park
715 South Foster Street
Dothan, 36302
(205) 794-3102
$7.00 for credit report with no
  rejection.

Trans Union Credit Information Co.
Mobile Division
605 Bel Air Blvd.
Mobile, 36606
(205) 471-5387
$8.50 for credit report with no
    rejection, including adding
    additional trade lines.

Credit Bureau of Montgomery
(CBD affiliate)
(Central Alabama Area)
435 S. McDonough St.
P.O. Drawer 830
Montgomery, 36112
(205) 834-2710
$5.00 for credit report, $6.00 for
    consumer file update.

Merchants Credit Association
2119 1st Ave., North
P.O. Box 10286
Birmingham 35202
(205) 252-7121
$7.00 for file review; $7.00 for any
    local additions or updates; $10.00
    for out-of-state or area changes.

Credit Bureau of Huntsville, Alabama
807 Franklin St. S.E.
P.O. Drawer E
Huntsville, 35804
(205) 533-9310
$4.50 for credit report if not rejected;
    $5.00 for report and review; $8.00
    plus toll charges if out-of-town for
    adding trade lines.

Credit Bureau of Mobile
118 N. Royal St. #202
P.O. Box 2167
Mobile 36652
(205) 433-5554
$7.50 for credit report and interview
    plus adding any trade lines.

ALASKA

Credit Bureau of Alaska
3400 Spenard Rd., Ste. 6
P.O. Box 4-C
Anchorage 99509
(907) 279-5689
$10.00 for credit report; no charge for
    adding trade lines.

Interior Credit Bureau, Inc.
910 College Rd.
P.O. Box 1619
Fairbanks 99707
(907) 452-2157
$12.50 for credit file review if not
    turned down; 2 credit references
    added for $3.00; $25-30 for
    complete update.

Juneau Credit Service Co.
197 S. Franklin #202
Juneau 99801
(907) 586-1300
$10.00 for credit report; no charge for
    adding trade lines.

ARIZONA

Credit Bureau Services of Arizona
    (Chilton)
100 W. Washington #1330
Phoenix 85003
(602) 252-0757, 258-5328
$5.00 for individual credit report and
    review, $7.50 for a couple with no
    rejection within 45 days; $7.50 for
    updating consumer file including
    additional trade lines, $8.50 for a
    couple.

Credit Data of Arizona, Inc.
(TRW System)
705 N. First St.
P.O. Box 2070
Phoenix 85001
(602) 252-6951
No charge for verbal disclosure; $5.00
    for copy of report; no charge for
    adding trade lines.

Credit Bureau Services of Arizona
    (Chilton)
5151 E. Broadway, Suite 420
Tucson 85711
(602) 745-8105
$5.00 for individual credit report and
    review, $7.50 for a couple with no
    rejection; $7.50 for updating consum-
    er file including additional trade
    lines, $8.50 for a couple.

ARKANSAS

Credit Bureau of Fort Smith, Inc.
513 Garrison Ave.

P.O. Box 1707
Fort Smith 72902
(501) 782-8861
$5.00 for credit report if not rejected;
  $5.00 for credit report transfer; no
  charge for updating file.

Credit Bureau Services (Chilton)
Plaza West Building, Suite 260
McKinley & Lee Streets
P.O. Box 1002
Little Rock 72203
(501) 661-1000
$5.00 for individual credit report
  review, $7.50 for couple with no
  rejection; $7.50 for updating in-
  dividual consumer file, $8.50 for a
  couple.

Credit Bureau Services (Chilton)
1500 Linden
P.O. Box 8228
Pine Bluff 71601
(501) 535-1130, 535-1133
$5.00 for individual credit report and
  review, $7.50 for a couple with no
  rejection; $7.50 for updating consum-
  er file, including additional trade
  lines, $8.50 for a couple.

CALIFORNIA

TRW Credit Data
1065 E. Hillsdale Blvd., Suite 400
Foster City 94404
(415) 571-1000
$8.00 for credit report with no
  rejection, including adding
  additional trade lines.

Trans Union Credit Information Co.
Southern California Div. (including
  L.A.)
1400 N. Harbor Blvd.
P.O. Box 3230
Fullerton 92635
(714) 738-3800
$8.00 for credit report with no
  rejection; $7.50 for 4 addi-
  tional trade lines; $2.00 for each
  additional line.

TRW Credit Data (Los Angeles area)
505 City Parkway West
Orange 92667
(714) 937-2000

24-hr. recordings: (714) 991-5100
                   (213) 254-6871
$8.00 for credit report with no
  rejection, including inserting
  additional trade lines.

TRW Credit Data
1300 E. Shaw Ave., Suite 147
Fresno 93710
(209) 226-5271
24-hr. recording: (209) 225-1998
$9.00 for credit report with no
  rejection, including inserting
  additional trade lines.

TRW Credit Data
966 Fulton Ave.
Sacramento 95825
(916) 481-9232
24-hr. recording: (916) 481-3115
$8.00 for credit report with no
  rejection, including additional trade
  lines.

Retailers Credit Association or RCA
  Credit Bureau of Sacramento
1801 J St.
P.O. Box 1318
Sacramento 95806
(916) 444-6811
$8.00 for a credit review including
  copy of file; $5.00 for 2 additional
  credit references.

Trans Union Credit Information Co.
Southern California Div. (Including
  San Diego)
770 B St., #40
P.O. Box 12069
San Diego 92112
(714) 232-6461

TRW Credit Data
2423 Camino Del Rio South
Suite 103
San Diego 92108
(714) 291-4525
24-hr. recording: (714) 296-0148
$8.00 for credit report if not rejected,
  including inserting additional trade
  lines.

Credit Bureau, Inc.
Credit Reporting Center San Jose
(serves San Francisco market and
  much of California)

6389 San Ignacio Ave.
P.O. Box 23016
San Jose 95119
(408) 224-2803
$7.00 for credit report if not rejected.

Credit Bureau of Santa Ana
1850 E. 17th St., #220
Santa Ana 92701
(714) 834-1685

Credit Bureau, Inc.
Santa Rosa Credit Reporting Center
50 Old Courthouse Square, Suite 301
Santa Rosa 95404
(707) 546-0551
$7.00 for credit report if not rejected.

COLORADO

TRW Credit Data
2260 S. Xanadu Way
Aurora 80014
(303) 695-4787, 695-8999
$8.00 for credit report if not rejected,
    including inserting additional trade
    lines.

Credit Bureau Services (Chilton)
(serves Denver and Boulder)
Suite 311-A
2323 S. Troy St.
Aurora 80014
(303) 695-0844
$5.00 for individual credit report and
    review; $7.50 for a couple if not
    rejected; $7.50 charge for updating
    consumer file, including additional
    trade lines; $8.50 for a couple.

Credit Bureau of Colorado Springs
(Chilton affiliate)
418 S. Weber
P.O. Box 26
Colorado Springs 80901
(303) 473-0960
$5.00 for individual or joint credit
    report if not rejected in last 45
    days; $4.50 for local individual
    update; $8.00 for 2 or more local
    updates. Outside of state $4.00 per
    city per state.

Pueblo Credit & Collection Bureau
425 W. 8th St.
Pueblo 81003
(303) 542-7554, 7550

CONNECTICUT

Credit Bureau, Inc.
Bridgeport Credit Reporting Center
144 Golden Hill St.
P.O. Box 484
Bridgeport 06601
(203) 366-7951
$7.00 for credit report if not rejected.

Credit Bureau Services (Chilton)
25 Pratt St.
P.O. Box 3398, Central Station
Hartford 06103
(203) 527-2601
$5.00 for individual credit report and
    review, $7.50 for a couple if not
    rejected; $7.50 for updating
    consumer file, including additional
    trade lines, $8.50 for a couple.

TRW Credit Data
211 State St., Rm. 418
Bridgeport 06604
(203) 384-0791
24-hr. recording: (203) 579-7857
$8.00 for credit report with no
    rejection, including additional trade
    lines.

Credit Bureau of Connecticut, Inc.
71 Elm St.
P.O. Box 1801
New Haven 06507
(203) 772-3420
$7.00 for credit report if not rejected
    plus $1.65 per trade line.

Credit Bureau Inc.
New London Credit Reporting Center
61 Bank St.
New London 06320
(203) 443-8941
$7.00 for credit report if not rejected.

DELAWARE

Credit Bureau of Del-Mar-Va, Inc.
106 W. Circle Ave.
P.O. Box 244
Salisbury, Maryland 21801
(301) 742-9551
$5.00 for credit report if not rejected
    and $1.00 per trade line.

DISTRICT OF COLUMBIA

Credit Bureau, Inc.
1345 University Blvd.
Langley Park, Maryland 20783
(301) 891-3000
$7.00 for credit report if not rejected.

TRW Credit Data
5565 Sterrett Place
Clark Bldg., Suite 527
Columbia, Maryland 21044
(301) 953-2360
24-hr. recording: (301) 596-4811
$5.00 for credit report with no
rejection, including additional trade
lines.

FLORIDA

Credit Bureau of Jacksonville
240 E. Duval St.
P.O. Box 52179
Jacksonville 32201
(904) 353-4801
$6.00 for credit report if not rejected
within 30 days.

Credit Bureau, Inc.
Miami Credit Reporting Center
14701 N.W. 7th Ave.
P.O. Box 680010
Miami 33168
(305) 685-8507
$7.00 for credit report if not rejected.

TRW Credit Data
1525 N.W. 167th St., Suite 320
Miami 33169
(305) 624-8471
24-hr. recording in English and
Spanish: (305) 625-7858
$8.00 for credit report if not rejected,
including inserting additional trade
lines.

Credit Bureau, Inc.
Orlando Credit Reporting Center
2250 Lee Rd.
Winter Park 32789
(305) 647-1400
$7.00 for credit report if not rejected
within 60 days; $2.50 per local
reference; $5.80 for 2 or more local
trade lines; $9.35 for out-of-state
trade lines.

Credit Bureau of Greater St.
Petersburg, Inc.
6666 22nd Ave., N.
St. Petersburg 33710
(813) 381-9686
$5.00 for credit report if not rejected;
$2.50 per reference.

Credit Bureau of Greater Tampa
(Trans Union affiliate)
134 South Tampa St.
P.O. Box 3307
Tampa 33601
(813) 273-7841
$8.00 for credit report if not rejected;
$3.00 for local trade lines; $7.00 for
out-of-area references.

GEORGIA

Credit Bureau, Inc.
Atlanta Credit Reporting Center
3 Executive Park Dr.
P.O. Box 95007
Atlanta 30347
(404) 329-1725
$7.00 for credit report if not rejected.

TRW Credit Data
6201 Powers Ferry Rd., Suite 200
Atlanta 30339
(404) 953-9265
24-hr. recording: (404) 953-3743
$8.00 for credit report if not rejected,
including inserting additional trade
lines.

Credit Bureau of Columbus
(CBI Contract Bureau)
703 20th St.
P.O. Box 1598
Columbus 31994
(404) 327-0201
$5.00 for credit report if not rejected;
$1.50 for 1 trade reference, $3.00
for more than one reference plus
toll charges if any.

Credit Bureau of Macon
(CBI affiliate)
484 Mulberry St. Suite 270
P.O. Drawer 4185
Macon 31212
(912) 743-3771
$5.00 for credit report if not rejected;
$5.00 for file update.

HAWAII

Credit Bureau Services (Chilton)
1164 Bishop St., Suite 500
Honolulu 96813
(808) 536-3741, 536-7372
$5.00 for individual's credit report
and review, $7.50 for a couple if
not rejected within 45 days; $7.50
for update consumer file including
inserting additional trade lines,
$8.50 for a couple.

IDAHO

Credit Bureau, Inc.
Boise Credit Reporting Center
6100 Emerald Dr.
Boise 83704
(208) 376-2122
$7.00 for credit report if not rejected
within 30 days; $3.50 for first local
trade line; $7.50 for up to 4 local
trade lines; $1.90 for each
additional update plus toll calls.

ILLINOIS

Trans Union Credit Information Co.
Chicago Div.
444 N. Michigan Ave.
P.O. Box 11036
Chicago 60611
(312) 645-6028
$8.00 for credit report if not rejected
within 30 days; $7.00 for first 3
additional trade lines; $1.00 for
each additional line.

TRW Credit Data
1699 Wall St.
Mt. Prospect, 60056
(312) 981-9400
24-hr. recording: (312) 981-0295
$8.00 for credit report if not rejected,
including inserting additional trade
lines.

Credit Bureau of Decatur, Inc.
260 E. Wood St.
P.O. Box 1279
Decatur 62525
(217) 424-1200

Credit Bureau of Greater Peoria
330 S.W. Adams, Suite 1

Peoria 61602
(309) 671-0500

Credit Bureau of Rockford, Inc.
3920 E. State St.
Rockford 61108
(815) 229-1550

Credit Bureau of Springfield, Inc.
825 E. Carpenter, P.O. Box 202
Springfield 62705
(217) 544-4661

INDIANA

Credit Bureau of Evansville, Inc.
103 N.W. 2nd St., P.O. Box 3677
Evansville 47708
(812) 424-2461

Credit Bureau of Ft. Wayne, Inc.
315 Washington Blvd.
Ft. Wayne 46802
(219) 422-2240

Merchant Association of Indiana
42 N. Pennsylvania
Indianapolis 46204
(317) 633-1555

Credit Bureau, Inc.
Muncie Credit Reporting Center
1535 N. Walnut St.
Muncie 47303
(317) 289-1816
$7.00 for credit report if not rejected.

Credit Bureau, Inc.
New Castle Credit Reporting Center
1426 Broad St.
New Castle 47362
(317) 529-3230
$7.00 for credit report if not rejected.

Credit Bureau of South Bend-
Mishawaka
312 W. Colfax, P.O. Box 1757
South Bend 46634
(219) 236-5620

IOWA

Credit Bureau of Cedar Rapids, Inc.
200 SGA Bldg., P.O. Box 4291
Cedar Rapids 52407
(319) 365-0401

Credit Bureau of Greater Des Moines
505 5th Ave., Suite 600
P.O. Box 1817
Des Moines 50309
(515) 247-8900
$5.00 for credit report if not rejected;
    $10.00 for credit file update.

Chilton Corporation
Suite H-5
600 5th Ave.
Des Moines 50309
(515) 288-9130
$5.00 for individual credit report and
    review, $7.50 for a couple if not
    rejected within past 45 days; $7.50
    for updating consumer file,
    including inserting additional trade
    lines, $8.50 for a couple.

KANSAS

Credit Bureau of Topeka, Inc.
915 Kansas Ave., P.O. Box 2607
Topeka 66601
(913) 357-4411

Affiliated Credit Bureaus, Inc.
(Independent, serviced by Pinger)
201 Kaufman Bldg.
Wichita 67202
(316) 263-9161
$5.00 for current credit report; no
    charge for file update, including
    additional trade lines.

Affiliated Credit Bureaus, Inc.
212 South Market St.
Wichita 67202
(316) 263-9161
$5.00 to review file if no rejection,
    which includes written copy.

KENTUCKY

Lexington Credit Bureau
(Independent, serviced by Trans
    Union)
135 W. Main St., P.O. Box 934
Lexington 40588
(606) 233-3300
$3.00 for consumer interview, in-
    cluding updating file; $5.00 for
    interview update and hard copy of
    file.

Trans Union Credit Information Co.
Louisville Div.
455 River City Mall #1233
Louisville 40202
(502) 584-0121
$8.50 if not rejected within last 30
    days; no charge for additional trade
    lines.

LOUISIANA

Credit Bureau of Baton Rouge, Inc.
4950 Government, P.O. Box 1427
Baton Rouge 70821
(504) 926-9640

Credit Bureau Services (Chilton)
First National Bank Tower, #500
666 Jefferson
Lafayette 70501
(318) 237-1749
$5.00 for individual credit report and
    review, $7.50 for a couple if not re-
    jected within last 45 days; $7.50
    charge for updating consumer file,
    including inserting additional trade
    lines, $8.50 for a couple.

Credit Bureau Services (Chilton)
1811 Tower Dr.
Monroe 71201
(318) 387-1153
$5.00 for individual credit report and
    review, $7.50 for a couple if not
    rejected within last 45 days; $7.50
    charge for updating consumer file,
    including inserting additional trade
    lines, $8.50 for a couple.

Credit Bureau Services (Chilton)
1539 Jackson Ave., P.O. Box 24060
New Orleans 70184
110 Veterans Blvd. Annex
#200-A
Metairie 70005
(504) 838-8030
$5.00 for individual's credit report
    and review, $7.50 for a couple if
    not rejected within last 45 days;
    $7.50 charge for updating consumer
    file, including inserting additional
    trade lines, $8.50 for a couple.

Credit Bureau of Greater Shreveport
620 Crockett, P.O. Box 1107

Shreveport 71163
(318) 222-3276

MAINE

Credit Bureau of Greater Portland, Inc.
(Chilton Contract Bureau)
66 Pearl St., P.O. Box 32 DS
Portland 04112
(207) 772-3771
$3.00 for credit report if not rejected;
  $1.50 per trade line.

MARYLAND

Credit Bureau of Baltimore, Inc.
(CBI affiliate)
300 Cathedral St., P.O. Box 926
Baltimore 21203
(301) 332-4635, 4600
$5.00 for credit report if not rejected
  for credit within 30 days.

Credit Bureau of Del-Mar-Va
106 W. Circle Ave.
P.O. Box 244
Salisbury 21801
(301) 742-9551
$5.00 for credit report if not rejected
  and $1.00 charge additional per
  trade line.

TRW Credit Data
5565 Sterrett Place
Clark Bldg., #527
Columbia 21044
(301) 992-3000
24-hr. recording: (301) 992-3055
$5.00 for credit report if not rejected;
  no charge for additional trade lines.

MASSACHUSETTS

Credit Bureau Services (Chilton)
6 St. James Ave., P.O. Box 73
Boston 02116
(617) 423-6400, 423-7417
$5.00 for individual credit report and
  review, $7.50 for a couple's credit
  report if not rejected within last 45
  days; $7.50 charge for updating
  consumer file, including inserting
  additional trade lines, $8.50 for a
  couple.

Credit Bureau Inc. of Western Mass.
145 State St.

Springfield 01103
(413) 736-4511, 17
$8.00 for credit report if not rejected;
  no charge for additional trade lines.

TRW Credit Data
16 Lakeside Office Park
Wakefield 01880
(617) 246-2800
24-hr. recording: (617) 245-5150
$8.00 for credit report if not rejected;
  no charge for additional trade lines.

Worchester Credit Bureau, Inc.
(Chilton affiliate)
1115 Mechanics Tower
Worcester 01608
(617) 756-1561, 1567
$5.00 for copy of credit report if not
  rejected; $2.00 per additional trade
  line; $5.00 for 3 or more additional
  trade lines.

MICHIGAN

Retailers' Credit Bureau, Inc.
3201 S. Dort Hwy.
Flint 48507
(313) 742-4000
$10.00 for credit report if not
  rejected, including updating
  consumer file.

Credit Bureau of Metro Grand Rapids
(Independent, serviced by Trans
  Union)
1155 Front Ave., N.W.
Grand Rapids 49504
(616) 456-6544
$5.00 for a copy of credit report if not
  rejected; $1.50 per trade line added
  to credit file.

Credit Bureau of Greater Lansing
(Chilton affiliate)
520 S. Washington, P.O. Box 40297
Lansing 48901
(517) 487-6561
$5.00 for oral interview; $8.00 for
  written report if not rejected; $6.00
  for oral interview for couples; $9.00
  for written report; $1.50 for local
  reference; $6.00 out-of-town ref-
  erence.

TRW Credit Data
P.O. Box 321

24450 Evergreen Rd.
Southfield 48037
(313) 352-6450
24-hr. recording: (313) 357-5320
$8.00 for credit report if not rejected;
no charge for additional trade lines.

MINNESOTA

Credit Bureau of Duluth-Superior, Inc.
(Pinger affiliate)
21 E. Superior St.
Duluth 55802
(218) 722-2861
$7.00 for credit report if not rejected,
including consumer file update.

Credit Bureau of Minneapolis
700 Plymouth Bldg.
Minneapolis 55502
(612) 370-9292

Credit Bureau Services (Chilton)
300 Midwest Bldg.
St. Paul 55101
(612) 298-6600, 6606, 6555
$5.00 for individual credit report and
review, $7.50 for a couple's credit
reports if not rejected within last 45
days; $7.50 for updating consumer
file, including inserting additional
trade lines, $8.50 for a couple.

MISSISSIPPI

Credit Bureau, Inc.
Gulfport/Biloxi Credit Reporting
Center
Security Savings & Loan Bldg.
2301 14th St., 5th Fl.
Gulfport 39501
(601) 863-7171
$7.00 for credit report if not rejected.

Credit Bureau, Inc.
Jackson Credit Reporting Center
200 E. Pascaquola
Jackson 39205
(601) 969-5570
$7.00 for credit report if not rejected.

Trans Union Credit Information Co.
Jackson Div.
514 S. President, P.O. Box 221
Jackson 39205
(601) 969-3430

$8.50 for credit report if not rejected;
$11.00 for report and any update
including additional trade lines.

Credit Bureau, Inc.
Natchez Credit Reporting Center
106 S. Wall St.
Natchez 39120
(601) 442-2841
$7.00 for credit report if not rejected.

Credit Bureau, Inc.
Tupelo Credit Reporting Center
1145 W. Main St.
Tupelo 38801
(601) 842-2424
$7.00 for credit report if not rejected.

MISSOURI

Credit Bureau of Greater Kansas
City, Inc.
906 Grand Ave., P.O. Box 476
Kansas City 64106
(816) 221-5600
$5.50 for interview and copy of credit
report if not rejected; $6.40 charge
for file update.

Trans Union Credit Information Co.
St. Louis Div.
408 Olive St., Suite 600
St. Louis 63102
(314) 241-4333
$8.50 for credit report if not rejected;
$2.00 charge for each additional
trade line.

Credit Bureau of Springfield
950 St. Louis St., P.O. Box 1325
Springfield 65805
(417) 862-3711

MONTANA

Credit Bureau of Billings
209 Stapleton Bldg., P.O. Box 1019
Billings 59103
(406) 259-3828

NEBRASKA

Credit Bureau Services of Omaha
(Chilton)
Collection Consultants, Inc.
4822 Dodge St., P.O. Box 31159
Omaha 68132
(402) 554-9600

$5.00 for individual's credit report and review, $7.50 for a couple's credit reports if not rejected within last 45 days; $7.50 charge for updating consumer file, including inserting additional trade lines, $8.50 for a couple.

NEVADA

Credit Bureau of Southern Nevada, Inc.
(Trans Union Contract Bureau)
1055 E. Tropicana, P.O. Box 19060
Las Vegas 89132
(702) 736-2951, 2949, 2940
$8.00 for credit report if not rejected for credit, including file update.

TRW Credit Data
1105 S. 8th St.
Las Vegas 89104
(702) 382-7031
$8.00 for credit report if not rejected; no charge for additional trade lines.

TRW Credit Data
495 Apple St., #110
Reno 89502
(702) 329-3106
24-hr. recording: (702) 825-0252
$8.00 for credit report if not rejected; no charge for additional trade lines.

NEW HAMPSHIRE

Credit Bureau Services of New Hampshire
(Independent, serviced by Chilton)
168 Manchester, P.O. Box 127
Manchester 03105
(603) 624-2629
$7.00 for copy of credit report and interview as well as any additional trade lines.

TRW Credit Data
16 Lakeside Office Park
Wakefield, Mass 01880
(603) 627-7583
24-hr. recording: (603) 627-7433
$8.00 for credit report if not rejected; no charge for additional trade lines.

NEW JERSEY

Credit Bureau Associates
(Independent, serviced by TRW)

817 Carpenter, P.O. Box 203
Camden 08101
(609) 541-4292
$9.00 for copy of credit report, including adding trade lines upon request.

TRW Credit Data
5 Century Dr.
Parsippany 07054
(201) 285-4840
24-hr. recording: (201) 285-4900
$8.00 for credit report if not rejected; no charge for additional trade lines.

Credit Bureau, Inc.
Tinton Falls Credit Reporting Center
(Serves New Jersey)
766 Shrewsbury Ave.
Tinton Falls 07724
(201) 842-7500
(800) 392-6807 toll-free in New Jersey
$7.00 for credit report if not rejected; $2.00–$10.00 for consumer file update.

NEW MEXICO

Credit Bureau of Albuquerque, Inc.
300 San Mateo, N.E. Ste. 500
Albuquerque 87108
(505) 265-1261
$2.50 for copy; $5.20 for interview and copy; $6.76 for entire file; $2.50 for additional trade line or update, $9.00 for complete update or $4.95 per trade line.

NEW YORK

Credit Bureau, Inc.
Albany Credit Reporting Center
3 Corporate Plaza
Washington Ave. Ext.
Albany 12203
(518) 869-6699, 2057
$7.00 for credit report if not rejected; $3.20 for first additional trade line; $7.05 for complete update.

TRW Credit Data
69 Delaware Ave., Suite 800
Buffalo 14202
(716) 849-1266
24-hr. recording: (716) 849-1288
$8.00 for credit report if not rejected; no charge for additional trade lines.

Credit Bureau, Inc.
Long Island/New York City
  Reporting Center
2234 Jackson Ave., 2nd Fl.
Seaford, L.I. 11783
(516) 785-5300
$7.00 for credit report if not rejected.

Trans Union Credit Information Co.
New York Div.
95-25 Queens Blvd.
Rego Park 11374
(212) 459-1800
$8.50 for credit report if not rejected;
  $1.50 charge per additional trade
  line.

TRW Credit Data
5 Century Dr.
Parsippany 07054
(212) 267-0981
24-hr. recording: (212) 233-8569
$8.00 for credit report if not rejected;
  no charge for additional trade lines.

TRW Credit Data
2450 Ridge Rd. West
Rochester 14696
(716) 225-3054
24-hr. recording: (716) 225-0585
$8.00 for credit report if not rejected;
  no charge for adding trade lines.

TRW Credit Data
299 S. Warren St., 4th Fl.
Syracuse 13202
(315) 474-1044
24-hr. recording: (315) 474-1048
$8.00 for credit report if not rejected;
  no charge for adding trade lines.

Credit Bureau Reports
(Serves all of western New York)
1040 Payne Ave.
North Tonawanda 14120
(716) 692-4421
$4.50 for credit report if not rejected.

NORTH CAROLINA

Credit Bureau of Charlotte, Inc.
(CBI System affiliate)
1515 Mockingbird #512
P.O. Box 34488
Charlotte 28234
(704) 525-9943

Credit Bureau of Greensboro
(CBI System affiliate)
210 W. Friendly, P.O. Drawer A
Greensboro 27401
(919) 373-1200
$5.00 for credit report if not rejected;
  $2.00 for first additional trade line;
  $10.00 for complete update.

Credit Bureau, Inc.
Raleigh Credit Reporting Center
5000 Falls of Neuse Rd.
P.O. Drawer 26868
Raleigh 27611
(919) 876-1460
$7.00 for credit report if not rejected;
  free updates or additions if rejected
  for insufficient credit data; $3.20
  for first additional trade line; $7.05
  for complete update.

Credit Bureau of Winston-Salem
514 First Union National Bank Bldg.
P.O. Box 3136
Winston-Salem 27102
(919) 725-7292
$2.00 for a review of a person's file if
  not rejected. No copies of credit
  report made available.

NORTH DAKOTA

Credit Bureau of Grand Forks
(Pinger System affiliate—Credit
  Bureau Data)
11 S. 4th St., P.O. Box 246
Suite B-2
Grand Forks 58201
(701) 775-8165
$5.00 for credit report if not rejected;
  no charge for in-person trade line
  additions.

OHIO

Akron Credit Bureau, Inc.
2641 W. Market St., P.O. Box 5426
Akron 44313
(216) 867-0780
$7.00 for credit report if not rejected
  within 30 days, no charge for
  simple, single update; $10.00 for
  credit update.

Credit Bureau of Cincinnati, Inc.
309 Vine St., P.O. Box 1239

Cincinnati 45201
(513) 651-6200, 6208
$8.00 for credit report if not rejected
within last 30 days; no charge for
in-person update if turned down for
insufficient credit data.

Credit Bureau Services of
Northeastern Ohio
666 Euclid Ave.
Cleveland 44114
(216) 579-3498
$8.00 for interview and copy of credit
report if not rejected.

Credit Bureau of Columbus, Inc.
(Pinger System affiliate)
170 E. Town St.
Columbus 43215
(614) 222-5327
$3.00 for copy of credit report if not
rejected; $8.00 for interview and
copy; no charge for additional trade
lines.

Trans Union Credit Information Co.
Dayton Div.
115 E. 3rd St., P.O. Box 698
Dayton 45402
(513) 223-6131
$8.50 for credit report if not rejected;
no charge for local trade line
additions; $6.00 if toll calls are
involved.

Credit Bureau of Toledo, Inc.
(Serviced by Trans Union)
626 Madison Ave. #500
Toledo 43604
(419) 244-1991
$7.50 for a consumer interview; $2.00
for copy of report at that time;
$7.50 for copy of credit report by
mail; $1.25 per trade line (local)
added; $10.00 deposit required for
out-of-town file information.

OKLAHOMA

Credit Bureau of Oklahoma City
(Serviced by Chilton)
2519 N.W. 23rd St.
Oklahoma City 73107
$7.00 to review file if no rejection,
which includes copy; $3.00 for each
local trade line; $20.00 for each
out-of-town bureau contacted.

(405) 947-6611
$7.00 for copy of credit report if not
rejected in last 30 days.

Credit Bureau of Tulsa
615 S. Detroit, P.O. Box 3424
(Serviced by Pinger)
Tulsa 74101
(918) 587-1261
$10.00 for copy of credit report if not
rejected; $8.00 for file update.

OREGON

Credit Bureau, Inc.
Portland Regional Credit Reporting
921 S.W. Washington, P.O. Box 4262
Portland 97208
(503) 222-6463
$7.00 for credit report if not rejected.

TRW Credit Data
9570 S.W. Barbur, Suite 311
Portland 97219
(503) 254-1352
$8.00 for credit report if not rejected;
no charge for trade line additions.

PENNSYLVANIA

Associated Credit Bureau Service, Inc.
(Independent, serviced by Trans
Union)
739 Hamilton Mall, P.O. Box 1640
Allentown 18105
(215) 820-6828
$3.00 for a copy of credit file in
person only; $7.00 for interview if
not rejected; $3.00–$5.00 for credit
file update.

Credit Bureau of Erie, Inc.
115 W. 11th St., P.O. Box 128
Erie 16501
(814) 454-5221

Trans Union Credit Information Co.
Philadelphia Div.
1211 Chestnut St., 10th Fl.
Philadelphia 19107
(215) 864-7834
$8.50 for credit report if not rejected;
$2.00 charge per trade line added.

Credit Bureau, Inc.
(Independent serviced by TRW)
908 Penn Ave., P.O. Box 596 (15230)
Pittsburgh 15222

(412) 288-1164, 1166
$10.00 for 2 copies of credit report;
no charge for update.

Credit Bureau of Scranton &
Lackawanna Counties
(Independent, serviced by TRW)
420 Connell Bldg.
Scranton 18503
(717) 344-7191
$8.00 for credit report and interview
if not rejected, including file update.

RHODE ISLAND

Credit Bureau of Greater Providence
(Independent, serviced by Chilton)
40 Fountain St., P.O. Box 1366
Providence 02901
(401) 273-7500
$6.00 for credit report if not rejected;
consumer must get creditors to
corroborate for additional trade
lines.

SOUTH CAROLINA

Credit Bureau, Inc.
Columbia Credit Reporting Center
223 Stoneridge Dr., Suite 1
Columbia 29202
(803) 256-2206
$7.00 for credit report if not rejected;
$3.20 for 1 local reference; $7.05
for up to 4 local credit references;
$1.90 each additional; $11.35 plus
tolls for multiple out-of-state credit
references; $6.05 plus toll for 1 out-
of-state reference.

SOUTH DAKOTA

Credit Bureau
317½ S. Phillips, P.O. Box 1403
Sioux Falls 57101
(605) 336-0470

TENNESSEE

Credit Bureau of Chattanooga
(Independent, serviced by Chilton)
501 Cherry St., P.O. Box 1030
Chattanooga 37401
(615) 265-8551

$2.00 for an in-person interview (no
copies given) if not rejected for
credit; $3.00 for local trade line
additions; $7.50 for out-of-town
credit references; $11.00 for a
couple.

Credit Bureau of Knoxville, Inc.
(Independent, serviced by Chilton)
1 Regency Square #340
P.O. Box 830
Knoxville 37901
(615) 546-1820
$4.00 for an oral review or $4.00 for a
written copy for an individual or
couple; $5.50 for file update.

Memphis Consumer Credit
Association, Inc.
#900, 2670 Union Ave. Extended
Memphis 38112
(901) 452-6580, 5991

Credit Bureau, Inc.
Morristown Credit Reporting Center
1758 W. Andrew Johnson Hwy.
Morristown 37814
(615) 586-5301
$7.00 for credit report if not rejected.

Credit Bureau of Nashville
(Independent, serviced by Chilton)
604 4th Ave., N.
P.O. Box 2563
Nashville 37219
(615) 254-7761
$5.00 for a copy of credit report;
$6.00 for a local update; $12.00 for
out-of-town update.

TEXAS

Merchants & Professional Credit
Bureau, Inc.
400 E. Anderson LN #520
P.O. Box 1623
Austin 78752
(512) 835-1890

Credit Bureau of Greater Corpus
Christi
509 Lawrence St., P.O. Box 1269
Corpus Christi 78403
(512) 884-2851

Credit Bureau Services (Chilton)
12606 Greenville Ave., P.O. Box 2049
Dallas 75243

(214) 699-6111, 6381
$5.00 for individual's credit report
and review, $7.50 for a couple's
credit reports if not rejected within
last 45 days; $7.50 charge for
updating consumer file including
inserting additional trade lines.

Credit Bureau Services (Chilton)
102 W. Oak, Suite G
Denton 75201
(817) 430-3221
$5.00 for individual's credit report
and review, $7.50 for a couple's
credit reports if not rejected within
last 45 days; $7.50 charge for
updating file, including inserting
additional trade lines.

Credit Bureau of El Paso, Inc.
1817 Wyoming, P.O. Box 942
El Paso 79946
(915) 545-1700

Credit Bureau Services (Chilton)
3345 Winthrop St.
Ft. Worth 76116
(817) 732-8851
$5.00 for individual credit report and
review, $7.50 for a couple's credit
reports if not rejected within the
last 45 days; $7.50 charge for
updating file, including inserting
additional trade lines.

Credit Bureau of Greater Houston
2505 Fannin St.
Houston 77002
(713) 652-3239

Chilton Corporation
11251 N.W. Freeway
Suite 215
Houston 77092
(713) 956-2088
$5.00 for individual credit report and
review, $7.50 for a couple's credit
report if not rejected within the last
45 days; $7.50 charge for updating
consumer file, including inserting
additional trade lines.

San Antonio Retail Merchants
Association
306 W. Market St.
San Antonio 78205
(512) 225-6461

UTAH

Credit Bureau of Salt Lake City
295 Jimmy Doolittle Rd.
Salt Lake City 84116
(801) 355-5905

VERMONT

Credit Bureau Services of Vermont,
Inc.
(Chilton affiliate)
230 College St., P.O. Box 56
Burlington 05402
(802) 863-5501, 2589
$7.00 for a credit report if not denied
credit; $1.00 charge per trade line.

VIRGINIA

Retail Merchants of Tidewater
Association
(Independent, serviced by CBI)
5755 Poplar Hall Dr.
P.O. Box 12736
Norfolk 23502
(804) 466-1600
$5.00 for credit report if not turned
down; $5.00 for file update.

TRW Credit Data
20 Koger Exec. Ctr. Set. 203
Norfolk 23502
(804) 461-4061   Norfolk
(804) 380-8992   Peninsual
$9.00 for credit report if not rejected;
no charge for additional trade lines.

Credit Bureau of Richmond, Inc.
700 E. Main St.
P.O. Box 1198
Richmond 23219
(804) 780-9345
$5.00 to review file if no rejection,
which includes copy; $3.50 per
trade line.

WASHINGTON

TRW Credit Data
2037 152nd Ave., N.E.
Redmond 98052
(206) 746-3881
$8.00 for credit report if not rejected;
no charge for additional trade lines.

Credit Bureau Services (Chilton)
521 W. Maxwell
P.O. Box 5393
Spokane 99205
(509) 455-5500
$5.00 for individual credit report and
review, $7.50 for a couple's credit
reports if not rejected within 45
days; $7.50 charge for updating
consumer file, including inserting
additional trade lines.

Credit Bureau of Tacoma
4009 Bridgeport Way W.
Tacoma 98466
(206) 565-6750

Credit Northwest Corp.
P.O. Box 2088
1601 Second Ave.
Seattle 98101
(206) 626-5500

WEST VIRGINIA

Credit Bureau of Charleston
P.O. Box 1707 (2nd Fl., Terminal
Bldg.)
Charleston 25382
(304) 343-2182

WISCONSIN

Credit Bureau of Green Bay, Inc.
130 E. Walnut St.
P.O. Box 460
Green Bay 54305
(414) 437-5995

Credit Bureau of Madison
(Independent, serviced by Trans
Union)
1400 E. Washington Ave. #233
P.O. Box 32
Madison 53701
(608) 256-1692
$3.00 for oral or in-person interview,
including local file updates; $5.00
for copy of credit report.

Credit Bureau of Milwaukee, Inc.
(Independent, serviced by Trans
Union)
414 E. Mason St.
P.O. Box 1996
Milwaukee 53201
(414) 276-6480
$5.00 for copy of credit report.

WYOMING

Credit Bureau of Casper
829 Cy Ave.
P.O. Box 970
Casper 82602
(307) 234-8901

Cheyenne Credit Bureau
213 W. 18th St.
P.O. Box 346
(307) 634-3511
$4.50 to review file if no rejection;
$7.50 for copy; $10.00 for trade
line.

Acceleration Clause.   A provision allowing the lender to ask for full payment immediately, if loan installments are not paid when due or for any other type of default.

Add-on Clause.   A provision allowing additional purchases on an existing installment credit agreement. This clause usually states that a default in making payments on additional purchases constitutes a default on all purchases.

Add-on Interest.   The total theoretical interest for the life of an installment loan, added to the principal at the outset and paid back along with the repayment of principal.

Adverse Action.   An action taken by a credit grantor that may include: (1) the refusal to grant credit in the amount or under the terms requested; (2) the termination of a credit account; or (3) a refusal to increase the amount of an existing credit line when it is requested in accordance with the credit grantor's procedures.

Amortization.   The paying off or "amortizing" of a loan in regular installments that include interest payments and partial repayments on principal.

Annual Percentage Rate (APR).   The finance charge on a loan over a one-year period, expressed as a percentage and reflecting the true costs of a loan as required by the Truth-in-Lending Act.

Appraisal Fee.   The charge for estimating the value of collateral being offered as security for a loan.

Appreciation.   The increase in value of an asset while it is being held.

Asset.   Any property of value that can be used to repay a debt. (See also *Current Asset, Collateral* or *Security.*)

Balance.   The amount left to pay on a loan as of a specific date.

Balance Sheet.   The listing of assets, liabilities, and net worth of a person, with the basic balance sheet equation being: assets − liabilities = net worth.

Balloon Payment.   Any lump sum payment that is more than the normal amount of any other regularly scheduled equal payment.

Bank Credit Card.   A credit card issued by a bank (such as VISA or MasterCard) that enables the borrower to buy goods and services or obtain a cash loan from banks honoring that card and paying later. (See also *Credit Card.*)

Bankruptcy.   The state of being unable to pay back one's debts (and freed from most of those debts), as determined by the action of a bankruptcy court. Voluntary bankruptcy is when the debtor takes the initiative; involuntary bankruptcy is when certain creditors take the initiative.

Billing Cycle.   The time interval (often one month) between regular billing statement dates.

Billing Error.   A mistake in a billing statement which may result from (1) a purchase made by someone not authorized by the credit card or charge card holder; (2) an arithmetic error; (3) a failure to reflect a credit; (4) a charge for which the cardholder requests clarification; or (5) other instances defined by the Fair Credit Billing Act and Regulation Z.

Cash Discount.   A price reduction offered by merchants to customers paying cash or by check instead of by credit or charge cards.

Cash Flow.   The net amount of cash left after all expenses, mortgage, and other debt payments have been made.

Charge Account.   A line of credit wherein goods or services may be purchased up to a specified limit, with payment usually due within 30 days of billing.

Charge Card.   A card (such as American Express or Diners Club) that operates on a pay-as-you-go basis within each billing cycle—not to be confused with a credit card, which allows customers to postpone complete payment as long as they continue to pay interest charges and at least part of the principal. (See also *Credit Card.*)

Charge-off.   An action taken by creditors, a bookkeeping loss on a loan because it has not been collected from the debtor in a reasonable period of time.

Chattel Mortgage.   A document that pledges one's non–real estate assets ("chattel" is an old term for personal property) as security for the payment of a debt.

Closing.   The final stage of document execution immediately preceding payment of loan proceeds to the borrower.

Closing Date.   The day of the month on which a credit card or charge card issuer calculates monthly bills—charges incurred after this date will be placed on the next month's bill. Also means the consummation of any financial transaction.

Closing Statement. The accounting of funds in any financial transaction.

Collateral. (See *Security*.)

Comaker or **Cosigner.** A person, other than the borrower, who signs a loan note or a purchase contract is equally or jointly responsible for its repayment. A cosigner gives additional protection to the creditor granting the loan because there is another source of repayment. (See also *Guarantor*.)

Commercial Banks. Federal or state-chartered corporations that provide a range of services, including checking accounts, savings, and time deposit accounts, consumer and business loans, mortgages, money exchange facilities, and trust management.

Community Reinvestment Act (CRA) Statement. A description available at each bank office for public inspection, showing what communities are served by that office and what types of credit the bank offers within those communities.

Comparison Shopping. The process of evaluating and comparing the annual percentage rate (APR) of each lender against the APRs quoted by other lenders.

Consolidation Loan. A loan that combines or "consolidates" several debts into a single loan. This type of loan usually reduces the actual dollar amount in payments each month by extending them over a longer period of time, but at a higher rate of interest. (See also *Refinance*.)

Cost Approach. Determination of the value of real estate by reconstructing the physical costs of the improvements and land.

Credit. An agreement to receive money, goods, or services now while paying for them in the future.

Credit Analysis. The process used by a credit grantor to evaluate a loan or credit card application.

Credit Bureau. A reporting agency that collects consumer credit information from businesses that extend credit and from public records and, in turn, sells this information back to its customers, who use such information to evaluate a consumer's credit standing or creditworthiness. Credit bureaus themselves do not grant credit.

Credit Card. A plastic card issued by a credit granting company, representing a type of account that allows the cardholder to obtain cash, goods, or services (within certain dollar limits) according to a "buy now, pay later" arrangement, as opposed to the pay-as-you-go arrangement of charge cards. (See also *Charge Card*.) Credit cards include those issued by banks, department stores, and gasoline, airline, and car rental companies. These cards allow customers to postpone complete payment each month as long as they continue to pay part of the principal plus interest charges.

Credit History. A record of a borrower's debt commitments and how well these commitments have been honored. An individual's credit history frequently is recorded on credit bureau reports. (See also *Credit Report* or *Profile*.)

Credit Investigation. An inquiry made by a credit grantor to verify information given by a borrower on a credit application.

Credit Life Insurance. Insurance that repays any unpaid portion of a loan in the event of a borrower's death.

Creditor. An individual or business that extends credit or lends money.

Credit Rating. The subjective evaluation of a person's credit history and creditworthiness.

Credit Report or **Profile.** A report assembled by a credit bureau that records an individual's credit history. (See also *Credit Bureau; Credit History*.)

Credit Risk. The perceived possibility of a loss incurred by a lender that would result from the nonpayment or delinquency of a borrower in repaying a debt.

Credit Scoring System. A statistical measuring system used by credit grantors to evaluate applicants by means of a point system, rather than by the human or subjective judgments of a credit officer. Based upon a creditor's previous experience with borrowers, a scoring system assigns certain points to attributes considered relevant to the creditworthiness of an applicant.

Credit Union. A cooperative organization owned and controlled by its members for the purpose of saving money and making this money available to members for loans.

Creditworthiness. The ability and willingness to repay debts.

Current Asset. An asset that is usually converted into cash within a year (such as inventory or accounts receivable).

Current Liability. An obligation to pay cash within a year.

Current Ratio. The ratio obtained by dividing current assets by current liabilities—a measurement of liquidity.

Debt Collector. Any person or collection agency, other than the creditor or creditor's attorney, that regularly collects debts for others.

Debt-to-Assets Ratio. An individual's total liabilities divided by his or her total assets—a measurement of solvency.

Debt-to-Equity Ratio. An individual's total liabilities divided by his or her owner's equity—a measurement of leverage. (See also *Equity; Leverage*.)

Debtor. An individual who uses credit, buying goods, services, or money under a promise of future payment.

Declining Balance. The decreasing amount owed on a debt as payments are made.

Default. The failure to meet any of the terms required by a credit agreement.

Defer. To delay payment or other action to a future time, for which a charge may be required.

Delinquent. The state of a credit account that is past due or irregular for any reason, and for which no satisfactory repayment or other arrangement has been made.

Depreciation.   The theoretical reduction of the bookkeeping value of an asset that reflects its declining usefulness in the creation of income.

Discharge of Lien.   The recorded release of a lien when debt has been paid. (See also *Lien*.)

Disclosure.   Information that a lender must give to a borrower before a credit contract is signed.

Discount Charge.   The total finance charge deducted in advance from a loan so that the money actually received by the borrower is less than the amount of the loan to be repaid. (See also *Finance Charges*.)

Discounting.   Determining the present value of a future amount of money—or the amount of money that must be invested today in order to receive a specified amount in the future.

Discretionary Income.   What remains of an individual's income after essential living expenses are paid.

Disposable Income.   An individual's net or take-home pay.

Down Payment.   The amount of money paid by the buyer to the seller at the time of the purchase.

Due Date.   The day of the month by which a payment must be made.

Earned Income.   Income from wages, salaries, or commissions that are subject to income tax.

Elderly Applicant.   A person age 62 or older, as defined in the Equal Credit Opportunity Act (1974).

Electronic Fund Transfer (EFT).   The movement of funds—for example, deposits, withdrawals, transfers, and debits to accounts—initiated by electronic means such as automated teller machines (ATMs).

Empirical Credit System.   See *Credit Scoring System*.

Escrow.   Funds held by a theoretically disinterested party.

Equity.   In real estate, the difference between the market value of a property and the debt against the property. (See also *Debt-to-Equity Ratio*.)

Equity Buildup.   The increase of equity created by the reduction of a debt secured by an asset. As the loan is reduced, the equity increases.

Equity Kicker.   Anything of value received by the lender in addition to interest.

Exit.   Lender's jargon for another source of repayment on a loan.

Extension.   An agreement with a lender that allows the borrower (who may be experiencing temporary financial difficulties) to make smaller payments on an outstanding debt over a longer term.

Finance Charges.   The cost of a loan in actual dollars and cents as required by the federal Truth-in-Lending Act (1968). In addition to the interest rate, finance charges can include loans fees, service charges, points, finder's fees, investigation fees, appraisal fees, and premiums for credit life insurance.

Finance Company.   A company that lends money or provides credit needed to purchase goods and services under installment payment agreements, often at a higher rate of interest than commercial banks, credit unions, or savings and loan institutions. (See also *Personal Finance Company* or *Personal Loan Company*.)

Financial Leverage. See *Leverage*.

Fixed Expenses. Expenses that are constant each month. Also known as "overhead."

Foreclosure. The act of "foreclosing" or selling of a property by a lender when the borrower has defaulted on a loan in which that property has served as collateral. (See also *Collateral* or *Security*.)

Garnishment. A court-sanctioned procedure that sets aside a portion of a debtor's salary or wages to repay creditors.

Grace Period. The time period after a loan payment's due date that is not subject to late charges.

Gross Income. Income collected from all sources—generally aggregate salaried income.

Guarantor. A person legally obligated to pay back a loan if the borrower defaults. A limited guarantor must pay only a specified amount. (See also *Comaker* or *Cosigner*.)

Hedge. (Against inflation.) Any investment effort or vehicle that helps protect against or lessen the effects of inflation.

Holder in Due Course. Someone who acquires in good faith and pays value for the obligation of another. (See also *Note* or *Promissory Note*.)

Inadvertent Errors. Unintentional errors resulting from mechanical, computer, or clerical factors.

Income Approach. The determination of a value based upon the capitalization of a stream of income. Capitalization rate is that rate at which investors are willing to invest their capital.

Inflationary Risk. The risk of loss in purchasing power of an investment dollar over a period of time.

Installment Sales Credit. A loan used to buy durable items such as automobiles and appliances whereby the buyer usually is required to make a down payment and repay the balance due (plus interest and service charges) in equal installments over a specified period of time. Installment loans usually involve a buyer, seller, and third-party lender, and are subject to special treatment by tax laws.

Instrument. A legal document, contract, promissory note, or written agreement.

Interest. One component of the finance charge for the use of credit or borrowed money—in a sense, the "rental price" of money. (See also *Simple Interest*.)

Joint Account. A credit arrangement for two or more persons that enables each person to use an account and jointly assume liability to repay debts.

Judgmental System. A nonstatistical, human, or subjective measure used by credit grantors to evaluate the creditworthiness of their applicants.

Land Contract. An installment contract drawn for the sale of property, occasionally used as a substitute for a mortgage, although ownership of a property does not exchange hands until the last installment is paid.

Late Charge. A percentage of the payment due that is charged because the borrower has paid late or after the predetermined grace period. (See also *Grace Period.*)

Leasing. The use of an asset or property for a fee. One to whom property is leased (tenant) is a "lessee"; one who conveys property or gives a lease (landlord) is a "lessor."

Leverage. The using of other people's funds to acquire assets.

Liability. Any responsibility that may be enforced by law.

Licensed Lender. A consumer finance office authorized to operate in the state where it is located.

Lien. A creditor's right to recover any debt out of specific assets of the debtor. A lien can be voluntarily given at the onset of the loan to assure repayment.

Line of Credit. The dollar amount of credit a lender makes available to a borrower, which may or may not be used by that borrower.

Liquidity. The rapidity with which a noncash asset can be converted to cash.

Liquidity Risk. The possibility of being unable to convert an asset to cash when needed.

Loan-to-Value Ratio. A loan expressed as a percentage of the overall value of the investment on which the loan is made. (See also *Debt-to-Equity Ratio.*)

Maturity. The time period allowed for full repayment of a loan; the maturity date is the date on which final payment is due.

Mortgage. A legal document creating a lien on property that has been pledged as collateral to ensure the repayment of an obligation; the covering. (See also *Lien, Security* or *Collateral.*) The mortgagor is the borrower and the mortgagee is the lender. Most mortgages should be recorded at a public office to be enforceable.

Mortgage Loan Commitment. A written statement by a lender to grant a specific loan amount at a given rate over a certain term and secured by a specific property.

Mutual Savings Bank. A nonprofit savings institution owned by its depositors with services that include savings accounts, home mortgage and home improvement loans, and, in some cases, checking accounts.

Net Worth. The difference between an individual's total assets and total liabilities.

Note or **Promissory Note.** A written document that is legal evidence of a debt, promising payment of a specific amount of money (plus finance charges) on a certain date or on demand.

Obligation. A debt.

Open-End Credit or **Revolving Credit Account.** A credit arrangement used by many retail stores whereby customers may purchase goods on a continual basis—up to a certain limit—and pay for all purchases within 30 days, or in stated monthly payments, based on the current account balance, plus interest on the unpaid balance.

Open-End Mortgage. A mortgage that can be restored to its original face amount after it has been paid down.

Opportunity Cost. The cost of foregoing other investment opportunities in order to keep a current investment.

Outstanding Balance. The unpaid portion of a loan.

Overdraft Checking. A line of bank credit permitting a person to write checks for more than the checking account balance, with interest charged on the amount borrowed—in effect, writing oneself a loan up to the limit of the credit line.

Paper. Jargon for a promissory note or other evidence of an obligation.

Passive Income. Nonsalary income, such as the income from interest, rents, royalties, dividends, and annuities.

Personal Finance Company or **Personal Loan Company.** (Often called a small-loan company or sales finance company.) A company that specializes in providing installment credit to individuals. (See also *Finance Company.*)

Personal Financial Statement. An individual's listing of personal assets, liabilities, and net worth on a specified date.

Personal Loan. (Also, a "signature loan" or "unsecured loan.") A loan granted on the signature of the borrower alone, without security. (See also *Security* or *Collateral.*)

Points. A loan discount—each point equaling 1 percent of the principal—that is used to adjust the yield on a loan in accordance with market conditions.

Prepayment Penalty. A charge imposed by the lender when the borrower pays back the loan in full before the maturity date. A prepayment privilege is a guarantee in the loan contract that there will be no penalty for early repayment in full.

Present Value. (Occasionally referred to as "discounting.") The amount of money that must be invested today in order to receive a certain amount in the future.

Prime Rate. The base interest rate on corporate loans at large U.S. money center commercial banks.

Principal. The amount of a loan before finance charges are deducted.

Proceeds. The net amount of cash received by the borrower at the closing of the loan transaction.

Purchase-Money Mortgage. A form of seller or owner financing in which the owner of a property makes a mortgage loan directly to the buyer with no bank involved as an intermediary.

Rebate. The portion of unearned interest returned to a borrower if the loan is repaid before maturity—the date designated for repayment.

Refinance. To revise the repayment schedule of an existing debt, usually extending the term and often increasing the interest charges.

Refund. A portion of a finance charge returned to the borrower, who pays off a loan before maturity. (See also *Rebate.*)

Repossession. The reclaiming by a seller of durable goods purchased on an installment credit plan when the buyer has fallen behind or defaulted on payments.

Rescission. The cancellation of a contract.

Reserve. Funds or assets set aside—such as money held by a lender to guarantee future payment for real estate taxes.

Return. The reward—usually expressed in percentages—anticipated from an investment.

Revolving Account. See *Open-End Credit* or *Revolving Credit Account*.

Risk. The possibility that expected returns will not be realized.

Rule of 78s. The formula by which many banks charge interest, stacking the interest at the front end of the loan, thereby penalizing a consumer who wishes to "prepay"—to pay off the loan early. (See also *Prepayment Penalty*.)

Sale and Leaseback. A transaction in which an owner of a property sells the property and simultaneously leases it back from the buyer, thus retaining use of the property, creating cash that otherwise would be locked up in equity, and perhaps creating some tax benefits.

Sales Finance Company. See *Personal Finance Company* or *Personal Loan Company*.

Savings and Loan Association. A federal or state-chartered thrift institution that pays interest to depositors (generally at a higher rate than the interest paid by commercial banks) and invests its funds primarily in real estate mortgages.

Savings Bank. A bank specializing in offering time deposit accounts to consumers and investing its deposits in real estate mortgages and bonds. (See also *Savings and Loan Association*.)

Scoring. See *Credit Scoring System*.

Second Mortgage. A lien that is secondary or junior to a first or prior mortgage. (See also *Mortgage*.)

Secured Loan or **Note.** A loan containing a provision that upon default certain property may be claimed by the lender, and sold, the proceeds to be applied to the payment of the debt.

Security or **Collateral.** Something of value (assets) pledged to assure loan repayment and subject to seizure and liquidation by the lender if the borrower defaults.

Seller Financing. See *Purchase-Money Mortgage*.

Service Charge. A charge activated by certain conditions of a credit contract, such as when overdraft checking is used.

Service Credit. A credit arrangement, used by utility companies and often medical professionals, that allows consumers to pay at the end of the month for services provided during the month.

Share Draft. A check-like instrument that enables credit union members to withdraw funds or pay bills from their interest-bearing or share accounts at a credit union.

Signature Loan. See *Personal Loan*.

Simple Interest. A method of calculating interest on an outstanding balance that produces a declining finance charge with each payment on an installment loan.

Single Lump Sum Credit. A closed-end credit arrangement in which the total outstanding balance is due on a specified date. (Also known as a "bullet.") (See also *Balloon Payment*.)

Statutory Fee. The administrative cost in closing a loan. (See also *Closing*.)

Surcharge. An increase in the normal price of an item.

Sweat Equity. Work done by the borrower (owner) to increase the value of a property.

Term. The total length of time allocated for the repayment of a loan.

Third-Party Transaction. A transaction that involves a buyer, seller, and lender (such as a conventional mortgage arrangement involving a bank as intermediary).

Title. Legal ownership.

Title Search. A check of public records to ascertain the ownership of a piece of real estate.

Unsecured Loan. See *Personal Loan*.

Usury. The charging of an excessive or illegal rate of interest. Usury laws specify the maximum interest rate that may be charged on various types of loans.

Wage Assignment. An agreement allowing a creditor to collect a portion of a borrower's salary directly from his or her employer if payment is not made according to the credit contract.

Waiver. The giving up of one's rights to something.

Working Capital. The excess of current assets minus current liabilities. (See also *Current Asset; Current Liability*.)